HIROHITO

HIROHITO

Karen Severns

CHELSEA HOUSE PUBLISHERS
NEW YORK

EDITOR-IN-CHIEF: Nancy Toff
EXECUTIVE EDITOR: Remmel T. Nunn
MANAGING EDITOR: Karyn Gullen Browne
COPY CHIEF: Juliann Barbato
PICTURE EDITOR: Adrian G. Allen
ART DIRECTOR: Giannella Garrett
MANUFACTURING MANAGER: Gerald Levine

Staff for HIROHITO:

SENIOR EDITOR: John W. Selfridge
ASSISTANT EDITOR: Sean Dolan
COPY EDITOR: Terrance Dolan
EDITORIAL ASSISTANT: Sean Ginty
ASSOCIATE PICTURE EDITOR: Juliette Dickstein
PICTURE RESEARCHER: Lynne Goldberg
SENIOR DESIGNER: David Murray
ASSISTANT DESIGNER: Jill Goldreyer
PRODUCTION COORDINATOR: Joseph Romano
COVER ILLUSTRATION: Richard Martin

CREATIVE DIRECTOR: Harold Steinberg

3 5 7 9 8 6 4 2

Library of Congress Cataloging in Publication Data

Severns, Karen. HIROHITO.

(World leaders past & present)

Summary: A biography of the Japanese emperor who, following World
War II, approved a constitution that changed his role from divine ruler to
"symbol of the state" with political control going to elected
representatives.
1. Hirohito, Emperor of Japan, 1901–] —Juvenile
literature. 2. Japan—Emperors—Biography—Juvenile
literature. 3. Japan—History—Shōwa period, 1926—]—
Juvenile literature. [1. Hirohito, Emperor of Japan,
1901–] . 2. Kings, queens, rulers, etc. 3. Japan—History—
Showa period, 1926–] I. Title. II. Series.
DS889.8.S37   1988   952.03′3′0924 [B] [92]   87-26828

ISBN 1-55546-837-3
    0-7910-0574-7 (pbk.)

Contents

John Adams
John Quincy Adams
Konrad Adenauer
Alexander the Great
Salvador Allende
Marc Antony
Corazon Aquino
Yasir Arafat
King Arthur
Hafez al-Assad
Kemal Atatürk
Attila
Clement Attlee
Augustus Caesar
Menachem Begin
David Ben-Gurion
Otto von Bismarck
Léon Blum
Simon Bolívar
Cesare Borgia
Willy Brandt
Leonid Brezhnev
Julius Caesar
John Calvin
Jimmy Carter
Fidel Castro
Catherine the Great
Charlemagne
Chiang Kai-Shek
Winston Churchill
Georges Clemenceau
Cleopatra
Constantine the Great
Hernán Cortés
Oliver Cromwell
Georges-Jacques
   Danton
Jefferson Davis
Moshe Dayan
Charles de Gaulle
Eamon De Valera
Eugene Debs
Deng Xiaoping
Benjamin Disraeli
Alexander Dubček
François & Jean-Claude
   Duvalier
Dwight Eisenhower
Eleanor of Aquitaine
Elizabeth i
Faisal
Ferdinand & Isabella
Francisco Franco
Benjamin Franklin

Frederick the Great
Indira Gandhi
Mohandas Gandhi
Giuseppe Garibaldi
Amin & Bashir Gemayel
Genghis Khan
William Gladstone
Mikhail Gorbachev
Ulysses S. Grant
Ernesto "Che" Guevara
Tenzin Gyatso
Alexander Hamilton
Dag Hammarskjöld
Henry viii
Henry of Navarre
Paul von Hindenburg
Hirohito
Adolf Hitler
Ho Chi Minh
King Hussein
Ivan the Terrible
Andrew Jackson
James i
Wojciech Jaruzelski
Thomas Jefferson
Joan of Arc
Pope John xxiii
Pope John Paul ii
Lyndon Johnson
Benito Juárez
John Kennedy
Robert Kennedy
Jomo Kenyatta
Ayatollah Khomeini
Nikita Khrushchev
Kim Il Sung
Martin Luther King, Jr.
Henry Kissinger
Kublai Khan
Lafayette
Robert E. Lee
Vladimir Lenin
Abraham Lincoln
David Lloyd George
Louis xiv
Martin Luther
Judas Maccabeus
James Madison
Nelson & Winnie
   Mandela
Mao Zedong
Ferdinand Marcos
George Marshall

Mary, Queen of Scots
Tomáš Masaryk
Golda Meir
Klemens von Metternich
James Monroe
Hosni Mubarak
Robert Mugabe
Benito Mussolini
Napoléon Bonaparte
Gamal Abdel Nasser
Jawaharlal Nehru
Nero
Nicholas II
Richard Nixon
Kwame Nkrumah
Daniel Ortega
Mohammed Reza Pahlavi
Thomas Paine
Charles Stewart
   Parnell
Pericles
Juan Perón
Peter the Great
Pol Pot
Muammar el-Qaddafi
Ronald Reagan
Cardinal Richelieu
Maximilien Robespierre
Eleanor Roosevelt
Franklin Roosevelt
Theodore Roosevelt
Anwar Sadat
Haile Selassie
Prince Sihanouk
Jan Smuts
Joseph Stalin
Sukarno
Sun Yat-sen
Tamerlane
Mother Teresa
Margaret Thatcher
Josip Broz Tito
Toussaint L'Ouverture
Leon Trotsky
Pierre Trudeau
Harry Truman
Queen Victoria
Lech Walesa
George Washington
Chaim Weizmann
Woodrow Wilson
Xerxes
Emiliano Zapata
Zhou Enlai

CHELSEA HOUSE PUBLISHERS

ON LEADERSHIP

Arthur M. Schlesinger, jr.

LEADERSHIP, it may be said, is really what makes the world go round. Love no doubt smooths the passage; but love is a private transaction between consenting adults. Leadership is a public transaction with history. The idea of leadership affirms the capacity of individuals to move, inspire, and mobilize masses of people so that they act together in pursuit of an end. Sometimes leadership serves good purposes, sometimes bad; but whether the end is benign or evil, great leaders are those men and women who leave their personal stamp on history.

Now, the very concept of leadership implies the proposition that individuals can make a difference. This proposition has never been universally accepted. From classical times to the present day, eminent thinkers have regarded individuals as no more than the agents and pawns of larger forces, whether the gods and goddesses of the ancient world or, in the modern era, race, class, nation, the dialectic, the will of the people, the spirit of the times, history itself. Against such forces, the individual dwindles into insignificance.

So contends the thesis of historical determinism. Tolstoy's great novel *War and Peace* offers a famous statement of the case. Why, Tolstoy asked, did millions of men in the Napoleonic Wars, denying their human feelings and their common sense, move back and forth across Europe slaughtering their fellows? "The war," Tolstoy answered, "was bound to happen simply because it was bound to happen." All prior history predetermined it. As for leaders, they, Tolstoy said, "are but the labels that serve to give a name to an end and, like labels, they have the least possible connection with the event." The greater the leader, "the more conspicuous the inevitability and the predestination of every act he commits." The leader, said Tolstoy, is "the slave of history."

Determinism takes many forms. Marxism is the determinism of class. Nazism the determinism of race. But the idea of men and women as the slaves of history runs athwart the deepest human instincts. Rigid determinism abolishes the idea of human freedom—

the assumption of free choice that underlies every move we make, every word we speak, every thought we think. It abolishes the idea of human responsibility, since it is manifestly unfair to reward or punish people for actions that are by definition beyond their control. No one can live consistently by any deterministic creed. The Marxist states prove this themselves by their extreme susceptibility to the cult of leadership.

More than that, history refutes the idea that individuals make no difference. In December 1931 a British politician crossing Park Avenue in New York City between 76th and 77th Streets around 10:30 P.M. looked in the wrong direction and was knocked down by an automobile—a moment, he later recalled, of a man aghast, a world aglare: "I do not understand why I was not broken like an eggshell or squashed like a gooseberry." Fourteen months later an American politician, sitting in an open car in Miami, Florida, was fired on by an assassin; the man beside him was hit. Those who believe that individuals make no difference to history might well ponder whether the next two decades would have been the same had Mario Constasino's car killed Winston Churchill in 1931 and Giuseppe Zangara's bullet killed Franklin Roosevelt in 1933. Suppose, in addition, that Adolf Hitler had been killed in the street fighting during the Munich *Putsch* of 1923 and that Lenin had died of typhus during World War I. What would the 20th century be like now?

For better or for worse, individuals do make a difference. "The notion that a people can run itself and its affairs anonymously," wrote the philosopher William James, "is now well known to be the silliest of absurdities. Mankind does nothing save through initiatives on the part of inventors, great or small, and imitation by the rest of us—these are the sole factors in human progress. Individuals of genius show the way, and set the patterns, which common people then adopt and follow."

Leadership, James suggests, means leadership in thought as well as in action. In the long run, leaders in thought may well make the greater difference to the world. But, as Woodrow Wilson once said, "Those only are leaders of men, in the general eye, who lead in action. . . . It is at their hands that new thought gets its translation into the crude language of deeds." Leaders in thought often invent in solitude and obscurity, leaving to later generations the tasks of imitation. Leaders in action—the leaders portrayed in this series—have to be effective in their own time.

And they cannot be effective by themselves. They must act in response to the rhythms of their age. Their genius must be adapted, in a phrase of William James's, "to the receptivities of the moment." Leaders are useless without followers. "There goes the mob," said the French politician hearing a clamor in the streets. "I am their leader. I must follow them." Great leaders turn the inchoate emotions of the mob to purposes of their own. They seize on the opportunities of their time, the hopes, fears, frustrations, crises, potentialities. They succeed when events have prepared the way for them, when the community is awaiting to be aroused, when they can provide the clarifying and organizing ideas. Leadership ignites the circuit between the individual and the mass and thereby alters history.

It may alter history for better or for worse. Leaders have been responsible for the most extravagant follies and most monstrous crimes that have beset suffering humanity. They have also been vital in such gains as humanity has made in individual freedom, religious and racial tolerance, social justice, and respect for human rights.

There is no sure way to tell in advance who is going to lead for good and who for evil. But a glance at the gallery of men and women in *World Leaders—Past and Present* suggests some useful tests.

One test is this: Do leaders lead by force or by persuasion? By command or by consent? Through most of history leadership was exercised by the divine right of authority. The duty of followers was to defer and to obey. "Theirs not to reason why / Theirs but to do and die." On occasion, as with the so-called enlightened despots of the 18th century in Europe, absolutist leadership was animated by humane purposes. More often, absolutism nourished the passion for domination, land, gold, and conquest and resulted in tyranny.

The great revolution of modern times has been the revolution of equality. The idea that all people should be equal in their legal condition has undermined the old structure of authority, hierarchy, and deference. The revolution of equality has had two contrary effects on the nature of leadership. For equality, as Alexis de Tocqueville pointed out in his great study *Democracy in America*, might mean equality in servitude as well as equality in freedom.

"I know of only two methods of establishing equality in the political world," Tocqueville wrote. "Rights must be given to every citizen, or none at all to anyone . . . save one, who is the master of all." There was no middle ground "between the sovereignty of all and the absolute power of one man." In his astonishing prediction of 20th-century totalitarian dictatorship, Tocqueville explained how the revolution of equality could lead to the *"Führerprinzip"* and more terrible absolutism than the world had ever known.

But when rights are given to every citizen and the sovereignty of all is established, the problem of leadership takes a new form, becomes more exacting than ever before. It is easy to issue commands and enforce them by the rope and the stake, the concentration camp and the *gulag.* It is much harder to use argument and achievement to overcome opposition and win consent. The Founding Fathers of the United States understood the difficulty. They believed that history had given them the opportunity to decide, as Alexander Hamilton wrote in the first Federalist Paper, whether men are indeed capable of basing government on "reflection and choice, or whether they are forever destined to depend . . . on accident and force."

Government by reflection and choice called for a new style of leadership and a new quality of followership. It required leaders to be responsive to popular concerns, and it required followers to be active and informed participants in the process. Democracy does not eliminate emotion from politics; sometimes it fosters demagoguery; but it is confident that, as the greatest of democratic leaders put it, you cannot fool all of the people all of the time. It measures leadership by results and retires those who overreach or falter or fail.

It is true that in the long run despots are measured by results too. But they can postpone the day of judgment, sometimes indefinitely, and in the meantime they can do infinite harm. It is also true that democracy is no guarantee of virtue and intelligence in government, for the voice of the people is not necessarily the voice of God. But democracy, by assuring the right of opposition, offers built-in resistance to the evils inherent in absolutism. As the theologian Reinhold Niebuhr summed it up, "Man's capacity for justice makes democracy possible, but man's inclination to injustice makes democracy necessary."

A second test for leadership is the end for which power is sought. When leaders have as their goal the supremacy of a master race or the promotion of totalitarian revolution or the acquisition and exploitation of colonies or the protection of greed and privilege or the preservation of personal power, it is likely that their leadership will do little to advance the cause of humanity. When their goal is the abolition of slavery, the liberation of women, the enlargement of opportunity for the poor and powerless, the extension of equal rights to racial minorities, the defense of the freedoms of expression and opposition, it is likely that their leadership will increase the sum of human liberty and welfare.

Leaders have done great harm to the world. They have also conferred great benefits. You will find both sorts in this series. Even "good" leaders must be regarded with a certain wariness. Leaders are not demigods; they put on their trousers one leg after another just like ordinary mortals. No leader is infallible, and every leader needs to be reminded of this at regular intervals. Irreverence irritates leaders but is their salvation. Unquestioning submission corrupts leaders and demeans followers. Making a cult of a leader is always a mistake. Fortunately hero worship generates its own antidote. "Every hero," said Emerson, "becomes a bore at last."

The signal benefit the great leaders confer is to embolden the rest of us to live according to our own best selves, to be active, insistent, and resolute in affirming our own sense of things. For great leaders attest to the reality of human freedom against the supposed inevitabilities of history. And they attest to the wisdom and power that may lie within the most unlikely of us, which is why Abraham Lincoln remains the supreme example of great leadership. A great leader, said Emerson, exhibits new possibilities to all humanity. "We feed on genius. . . . Great men exist that there may be greater men."

Great leaders, in short, justify themselves by emancipating and empowering their followers. So humanity struggles to master its destiny, remembering with Alexis de Tocqueville: "It is true that around every man a fatal circle is traced beyond which he cannot pass; but within the wide verge of that circle he is powerful and free; as it is with man, so with communities."

1

The Voice of the Crane

At one minute to noon on August 15, 1945, life in Japan came to a standstill. Those with radios nervously tuned in to the Japanese national network, NHK; those without stopped, bowed to the loudspeakers that had been placed in the streets, and waited in awe for the unprecedented broadcast to begin.

The strains of the national anthem, *Kimigayo*, came over the airwaves at noon; when they faded out, an announcer intoned, "His Majesty the Emperor will now read the imperial rescript to the people of Japan." A recording — one of two made near midnight the night before and smuggled past conspirators — was played, and for the first time in their history the Japanese people heard their emperor address them.

"To Our good and loyal subjects," Emperor Hirohito began. He spoke in a nervous, high-pitched tone and used the imperial pronoun *Chin* to refer to himself. Translated as "we," Chin literally means "moon that speaks to heaven" and is used only by

We have spent 2 billion dollars on the greatest scientific gamble in history and won. If the Japanese do not now accept our terms they may expect a rain of ruin from the air, the like of which has not been seen on this earth.
—HARRY TRUMAN
U.S. president (1945–1953), after the dropping of the atomic bombs

Emperor Hirohito prepares to read an imperial order to the Diet, the nation's representative assembly, in 1945. Under Japan's pre–World War II constitution the emperor possessed almost absolute authority but was expected not to be active in the making of government policy.

Ancient metaphor likened the Japanese emperor to a crane watching over his kingdom from above the clouds.

the emperor. Hirohito continued: "After pondering deeply the general trends of the world . . . We have decided to effect a settlement of the present situation by resorting to an extraordinary measure. We have ordered Our Government to communicate to the Governments of the United States, Great Britain, China and the Soviet Union that Our Empire accepts the provisions of their Joint Declaration."

Long before the final exhortation — "Submit, ye, to Our Will!" — most of the listeners had ceased hearing the words. Millions of Japanese wept. The emperor's difficult, archaic language did not obscure his message. The ". . . war situation has developed not necessarily to Japan's advantage, while the general trends of the world have all turned against her interest," the emperor said, and his subjects understood. After the death of nearly 2 million soldiers and hundreds of thousands of civilians; the destruction of over 50 square miles of Tokyo, the nation's capital and largest city, and a portion of the imperial palace from U.S. bombing raids; and the utter devastation of the cities of Hiroshima and Nagasaki by atomic bombs, Japan was defeated. World War II was over. The emperor — likened in ancient metaphor to a crane watching over his people from on high — spoke of the future: "Unite your total strength. . . . Cultivate the ways of rectitude; foster nobility of spirit; and work with resolution so as ye may enhance the innate glory of the Imperial State and keep pace with the progress of the world."

Never in its long history had Japan been conquered by another nation, and not all of its military leaders were ready to accept defeat. Even as Hirohito had prepared his address the previous evening, soldiers led by Major Hatanaka Kenji had seized control of the imperial palace. The rebellion had been brewing for several days, since word had spread that the emperor and the cabinet were contemplating surrender. The conspirators sought to enlist the support of the war minister, Anami Korechika, and the local army commander, Mori Takeshi, but both men said that the decision to surrender had already been reached and that the emperor wished it so. But Japan was not yet defeated, the conspirators argued. The armed forces were prepared to fight to the last man. Japanese society prized loyalty — to family, to clan, to nation, to emperor — as the highest virtue.

Many of the buildings on the grounds of the imperial palace in Tokyo were destroyed by U.S. bombing raids during World War II. When the imperial residence itself was damaged, Hirohito and his family took shelter in the *obunko*, the imperial library.

Much of the city of Nagasaki was reduced to rubble when the United States dropped an atomic bomb there on August 9, 1945. An atomic bomb was first used against Hiroshima on August 6; the devastation of the two cities helped convince Hirohito that Japan should surrender.

Mori told Hatanaka that it was his duty as a loyal Japanese to obey the orders of the emperor. The emperor had been misled, Hatanaka replied. Traitorous defeatists among his advisers had counseled surrender. The true wishes of the emperor, and the best interests of the nation, would be served by further resistance. Mori delayed, unsure where to place his loyalty. Hatanaka drew his pistol and shot him through the chest. Anami, who had argued in cabinet meetings for continuing the war, had earlier retired to his home, unable to disobey the emperor and certain that the coup would fail. There he spent the night conversing with friends and relatives and drinking sake, the potent Japanese rice liquor. At dawn he committed the suicide rite of *seppuku* as an act of atonement for his role in the Japanese defeat. He left behind a brief poem as explanation:

> Believing in the eternity of our Divine Land,
> with my death I apologize to the Emperor
> for the great crime

Without Mori and Anami, the rebellion had little chance of success. The conspirators attempted to find the recordings the emperor had made in order to prevent his message from reaching the people, but they had been carefully hidden. Hatanaka halfheartedly attempted to take over the radio station on the morning of the 15th, but he was persuaded to give up the rebellion by a superior officer. Shortly before the emperor's address, Hatanaka shot himself. In the week that followed, nearly 800 Japanese military men committed suicide, but the surrender met with no further resistance.

The most trying hours of Hirohito's life began on August 9, 1945. That day the United States dropped its second atomic bomb, on Nagasaki, and the Soviet Union officially entered the war against Japan. The two events were equally devastating to the Japanese. Officials at Nagasaki put the death toll there at 75,000; thousands more would die of radiation sickness in the months and years to come. As Soviet troops moved into Manchuria — China's three northernmost provinces, which Japan had invaded in 1931 and held since — Japan's last chance for negotiating a peace faded. Until that point, Japan had hoped to lure the Soviet Union into mediating a peace with the United States and Great Britain that would enable Japan to avoid surrender and occupation and maintain its national sovereignty, using as bait its possessions in Manchuria and the Kurile Islands, which the Soviets had long coveted. But the Soviets, technically neutral in the Pacific theater of the war by virtue of a nonaggression pact signed earlier with Japan, had agreed to declare war on Japan at the July conference of the Allies at Potsdam, Germany. The Japanese offer was of little temptation to the Soviets, who recognized that Japan was on the verge of defeat and unable to prevent the Soviets from simply taking what they wanted.

The Japanese had never ruled out a negotiated peace as an end to their involvement in World War II, provided it could be made on terms that allowed them to keep some of the territory they had seized since the beginning of the war. World War II began in the Pacific with Japan's sneak attack on the U.S. naval base at Pearl Harbor, Hawaii, on December 7, 1941. By August 1942 the Japanese controlled Formosa (Taiwan), the Philippines, Laos, Vietnam, Cambodia, Thailand, Malaya, the Dutch East Indies (Indonesia), Borneo, New Guinea, and various

Prime Minister Konoye Fumimaro, Foreign Minister Matsuoka Yusoke, Navy Minister Yoshida Zengo, and War Minister Tojo Hideki deliberate in August 1940, shortly before Japan signed the Tripartite Pact with Germany and Italy. Hirohito's cabinet tried to persuade him that the agreement would ensure peace, but the Tripartite Pact made war with the United States inevitable.

island groups in the western Pacific. Hirohito believed that at that point Japan should negotiate an advantageous peace, and Japanese emissaries in Switzerland broached the subject through intelligence channels, but U.S. President Franklin Roosevelt had determined at the outset of the war that the United States would settle for nothing less than total victory over the Japanese. "We are going to win the war, and we are going to win the peace," Roosevelt said two days after the Pearl Harbor attack.

The Allied (the Allies were the United States, the Soviet Union, Great Britain, and France, although the Soviet Union was neutral regarding Japan until August 9, 1945) policy of pursuing the unconditional surrender of their enemies Japan and Germany (Germany was the aggressor in the European war, which began in 1939) had been first stated publicly by Roosevelt at a January 1943 conference with Prime Minister Winston Churchill of Great Britain at Casablanca, Morocco. At Potsdam in July 1945, U.S. president Harry Truman, who succeeded Roosevelt upon the latter's death in April, met with Soviet leader Joseph Stalin and Churchill and his

At Potsdam, Germany, in July 1945, British prime minister Winston Churchill (with cigar); his eventual successor, Clement Attlee (second to right of Churchill); Soviet leader Joseph Stalin (third to right of Attlee); and U.S. president Harry Truman (with glasses, opposite Attlee) reiterated the Allied policy of pursuing Japan's unconditional surrender.

successor, Clement Attlee, to discuss postwar arrangements in Europe. (Germany had been defeated in May.) While there, the Allied leaders reiterated their policy of unconditional surrender regarding Japan. The Potsdam Proclamation, which Stalin did not sign, also called for the elimination of "those who have deceived and misled the people of Japan into embarking on world conquest"; the occupation of Japan until its war-making ability was destroyed; the implementation of the terms of the Cairo declaration, which would strip Japan of all the territory it had seized since 1914 and restrict Japanese sovereignty to its four main islands; the total disarmament of the Japanese military; the punishment of war criminals and the establishment of a more democratic form of government; and the supervision of Japanese industry to enable it to recover but not rearm. The occupation of Japan would end when a peaceful and responsible government was established. Failure to comply would "mean the inevitable and complete destruction of the Japanese armed forces and just as inevitably the utter devastation of the Japanese homeland." The proclamation was issued on July 26, ten days after the first successful testing of the atomic bomb.

President Franklin Roosevelt of the United States (second from left) announced at Casablanca, Morocco, in January 1943 that the Allies would demand the unconditional surrender of Japan, Germany, and Italy. At Casablanca, Roosevelt met with Generals Henri Giraud (far left) and Charles de Gaulle (second from right) — the leaders of the Free French — and Churchill.

Henry Stimson was twice U.S. secretary of war, from 1911 to 1913 and from 1940 to 1945. In the final days of World War II Stimson argued that political alternatives to using the atomic bomb should be explored, even if it meant assuring the Japanese that they would be allowed to keep the emperor.

The Soviet Union's rejection of Japan's peace entreaties eliminated the last hope of Japan's leaders that an alternative to continued resistance or unconditional surrender could be found, and the use of the atomic bomb on Nagasaki demonstrated the cost of carrying on with the war. With the cabinet deadlocked on the question of surrender, Hirohito and Suzuki Kantaro, the prime minister, arranged to call a meeting of the Supreme Council for the Direction of the War, which was composed of the prime minister, war minister, foreign minister, navy minister, and army and navy chiefs of staff. The council met in a fortified bunker off the imperial library, the *obunko*, where Hirohito and his family had moved after their usual residence within the palace was damaged by the U.S. bombing raids.

Hirohito traced his lineage in a direct line to Jimmu Tennu, who was the first Japanese emperor and according to legend founded the Japanese nation in 660 B.C. Through Jimmu, Hirohito was also deemed to be directly descended from Amaterasu, the Japanese sun goddess. Jimmu was believed to be Amaterasu's grandson and was said to have been sent by her to take possession of the Japanese islands and establish an unending imperial dynasty. The mythology of Amaterasu and the divine origins of the imperial dynasty formed an integral part of the Japanese religion of *Shinto*, which is characterized by polytheism (belief in many gods) and ancestor worship. Shinto became the state religion at about the time the authority of the emperor was restored in 1868.

The emperor's right to rule was thus divinely sanctioned. He was seen as the very embodiment of Japan's national essence, or *kokutai*. As the restoration of the imperial authority foreshadowed Japan's remarkable transformation from an isolated, defenseless nation to a modern empire with vast colonial possessions, the identification of the emperor with kokutai grew even greater.

How to preserve kokutai in the face of the nation's impending defeat was the concern of the ministers and military men in the bunker of the obunko that night. Arguing against the surrender were Toyoda

Soemu, the navy chief of staff; Anami Korechika, the war minister; and Umezu Yoshijiro, the army chief of staff. Japan still had 2 million soldiers in uniform, and the entire nation was prepared to die in defense of the homeland. Even if ultimately defeated, the Japanese could still inflict great casualties on the Allies, Anami said. "Even if we fail [to defeat the expected Allied invasion], our hundred million people are ready to die for honor." Of great concern to the three opposing surrender were the provisions of the Potsdam Proclamation calling for the elimination and trial as war criminals of those responsible for Japan's wartime policy. Such trials would be likely to include themselves and friends, family members, and colleagues among Japan's political and military leadership. Of even greater consequence was the possibility that the victors would hold the emperor responsible for the nation's actions. To see the emperor tried as a criminal would

Jimmu Tennu (left) was the first Japanese emperor and was believed to be a descendant of Amaterasu, the sun goddess. Hirohito was the 124th emperor in an unbroken line dating back to Jimmu Tennu, but he discounted the myths of divine origin.

Hirohito's grandfather, Emperor Meiji, ruled Japan from 1867 to 1912. This period was known as the Meiji Restoration because it witnessed the reestablishment of the emperor's direct authority and Japan's modernization through conscious emulation of the Western nations.

be more unbearable than defeat. Even if the emperor were to escape trial, the insistence of the Allies on the democratization of the country might eliminate his role. In either case, kokutai would not be preserved.

Suzuki, the prime minister; Yonai Mitsumasa, the navy minister; and Togo Shigenori, the foreign minister, argued that there was no choice. The nation was unable to resist any further. There could be no question of preserving the national essence if there were no longer a nation. The wisest course would be to ask for peace with a minimum of counterdemands, the most important being that the emperor be allowed to remain.

As at the cabinet meeting earlier that day, and at the many meetings held in the prior weeks, no decision could be reached. After nearly three hours of debate, Suzuki took the unprecedented step of asking the emperor to intervene.

Although under Japan's constitution the emperor possessed virtually unlimited power — he opened, closed, and could dissolve the legislative assembly, was the supreme commander of the armed forces, declared war, concluded treaties, and was sacred and inviolable — his actual power and ability to act had been fixed by tradition, which held that he presided over but did not participate in the political processes of the nation. His approval was needed to make any decision of the cabinet official, but his approval was signified by his presence at the meetings where the cabinet reached its decisions. The emperor was expected to preside while the ministers argued their positions and reached a consensus, but never to indicate his own preferences. He was to remain unsullied by the day-to-day, petty, and partisan concerns of the government while looking out for the nation's greater interests. When one of Hirohito's ancient forebears had displayed an aptitude for or interest in practical politics, he resigned as emperor so that he could exercise his talents without staining the sanctity of the imperial office. Hirohito's authority derived from the respect and obedience every Japanese accorded him as the living embodiment of the country's national essence.

In a nation that had never known defeat by a foreign power, that had ended more than two and a half centuries of near total isolation from all manner of foreign influence less than 100 years before, the weight of tradition was very heavy indeed, but Hirohito did not hesitate. "I will state my opinion," he said. "I have concluded that to continue this war can only mean destruction of the homeland. I cannot bear to have my innocent people suffer any further. . . . I wish to hand the country of Japan to our descendants; I wish to see as many as possible of our people survive and rise again. . . . Disarmament of my brave and loyal men is painful to me. Painful, too, that my devoted vassals should be considered war criminals. . . . But the time has come to bear the unbearable."

The ministers and chiefs of staff wept. After regaining their composure, they agreed that the em-

It was the nation's [Japan's] good fortune that in spite of the existence of a hard-headed and strong-willed corps of fanatics, the men responsible for the movement to terminate the war were finally able to give the fullest possible effect to the depth of appeal in the voice of the man who is the supreme symbol of Japanese life and thought.
—DR. ROBERT C. BROWN
author, on Hirohito's
radio address

The arms of the emperor of Japan consist of the imperial dragon, the sacred phoenix, and the tortoise. These creatures are symbolically related to the royal house and are believed to protect the emperor and his domain.

peror's wish would become their unanimous decision. Hirohito had not issued an order; his desire to end the war had been expressed as "I wish," but it was as close to issuing an order to his cabinet as Hirohito had ever come. The ministers and chiefs of staff retired to Suzuki's house, where the entire cabinet assembled and was apprised of what the emperor had said. Notes were sent to each of the Allies, accepting the Potsdam Proclamation with the condition that acceptance did "not compromise any demand which prejudices the prerogatives of his Majesty as a Sovereign Ruler," or, in other words, that the emperor be allowed to remain.

Truman and his advisers were divided on Japan's response. Secretary of War Henry Stimson believed retaining Hirohito would be of practical use in effecting the surrender, as only the emperor would be able to persuade Japan's fighting men to actually lay down their arms. Secretary of State James Byrnes believed that acceptance of the Japanese message would constitute a retreat from the policy of unconditional surrender. It was the United States, not Japan, that should be setting conditions, Byrnes believed.

The U.S. response was written by Byrnes and approved by the Allies. Carefully worded, it was intended to reassure the Japanese about the future status of the emperor while reaffirming the policy of unconditional surrender, but it provoked another crisis in Japan. The authority of the Japanese government and the emperor to rule would be subject to the supreme commander of the Allied powers, the U.S. response said. The ultimate form of the Japanese government would "be established by the freely expressed will of the Japanese people."

The U.S. message reached Japan very early on the morning of August 12. The cabinet ministers were again divided, along the same lines as before. After two days of fruitless debate, another imperial conference was arranged, this time with the entire cabinet present. As at the August 9 meeting, the ministers noticed the emperor's obvious fatigue and disheveled appearance. Toyoda, Umezu, and Anami again stated their reasons for not approving the

As foreign minister in the war cabinet of 1941, Togo Shigenori pressed for a negotiated settlement to Japan's differences with the United States. As foreign minister in the surrender cabinet of 1945, Togo directed Japan's negotiations with the Soviet Union and counseled surrender when they failed.

Byrnes message. The emperor listened and then spoke. "If there are no more opinions, I will express mine. I want you all to agree with my conclusions," he said. Japan was unable to continue the war. The Allied note was acceptable and did not subvert kokutai. To continue the war would mean the destruction of the nation and the loss of hundreds of thousands of more lives, something he could not bear. Like his grandfather, the great Emperor Meiji, he must now bear the unbearable and endure the unendurable. As the ministers sobbed, Hirohito finished by saying that it was his desire that "all of you, my ministers of state, bow to my wishes and accept the Allied reply forthwith." He volunteered to inform the Japanese people of his decision and asked the cabinet to write an imperial rescript ending the war.

The next day at noon Hirohito's address was broadcast to the nation. Thirteen days later the first U.S. troops landed on the main Japanese island of Honshu, followed two days later by the supreme commander of the Allied powers (SCAP), General Douglas MacArthur, and for the first time Japan, in some ways the most xenophobic of nations, experienced life under a military occupation.

2

Descended from the Gods

Hirohito was born to Crown Prince Yoshihito and Crown Princess Sadako in Tokyo on April 29, 1901. When Hirohito was only 70 days old, he was entrusted to the foster care of Count Kawamura Sumiyoshi. Japanese royal infants traditionally spent their earliest years in the care of a respected member of the nobility, who considered it a great honor to be entrusted with such a duty.

Originally initiated to protect the royal heirs from ambitious plotters at court, the practice had been continued so that the royal infants would spend some of their youth away from the rarefied atmosphere of the imperial palace and enjoy a somewhat more "normal" upbringing for the earliest portion of their lives. It was hoped that the practice would also serve to protect the royal children from the illnesses that claimed so many of the heirs. For example, four of Yoshihito's half-brothers had died young, and Yoshihito was not in the best of health.

Hirohito was alarmingly puny at birth and his mother would be unlikely to enlist any expert or effective medical help should he fall ill. For princely bodies were sacrosanct in those days and no doctor could touch them, let alone give them injections.
—LEONARD MOSLEY
author, on
Hirohito's infancy

Worshipers at a Shinto temple in Kyoto, the imperial capital until 1869. With its emphasis on ancestor worship and the divine origins of Japan and the royal line, Shinto was traditionally associated with those who favored strong imperial authority. It was the state religion during the Meiji Restoration.

Hirohito's father, Yoshihito, took the reign name Taisho, meaning Great Righteousness, when he took the throne on the death of Meiji in 1912. But his mental illness left him incapable of the subtle exercise of power at which Meiji had been so adept.

Count Kawamura was a vice-admiral and a member of the Privy Council, the emperor's inner circle of advisers. The conflict between the modern and the traditional, or the search to adopt those modern ideas and methods that would enable Japan to strengthen itself without losing its distinctive identity, has been the dominant theme in Japanese history since the mid-19th century. Like so many Japanese of his age and class, Kawamura, who was 65 years old when Hirohito came to live with him, mixed both the traditional and modern in his life.

In the early 1600s Japan entered a period of self-imposed isolation known as *sakoku*, which was intended to rid the country of all aspects of Western influence, particularly Christianity, which had made inroads with the arrival of Portuguese, Dutch, and British traders in the previous century. Japan expelled the foreigners and closed itself to the world. Only rarely were Japanese allowed to travel to foreign lands. This isolation was to last until July 1853, when Commodore Matthew Perry of the United States and his fleet of two gunships and two steamers weighed anchor in the port of Uraga. After some mutually unsatisfactory meetings with Japanese delegates, the "black ships" left, but they returned the following year. Their coming marked the end of sakoku. Japan was induced to sign trade agreements with the United States, then with Russia, Great Britain, the Netherlands, and other European powers. The coming of the black ships also demonstrated to the Japanese how weak and stagnant their nation had grown in the past two centuries, as illustrated by their inability to simply turn away the foreigners. It was evident that the West was far more advanced than Japan, particularly in terms of military strength. This revelation was the catalyst for the adaptation of Western methods and technology that enabled Japan to rebuild its military strength and begin challenging European nations for Asian territories and resources by 1900.

Kawamura had played his part in that process. In the 1870s he had arranged for British naval officers to train the developing Japanese navy, yet at home

The empress Sadako, Hirohito's mother, lived in seclusion in the imperial palace in Tokyo. Her children were raised by trusted advisers and lived in their own palaces scattered around the imperial grounds.

he lived in traditional Japanese fashion. While Hirohito's father succumbed to the Japanese enthusiasm for Western ideas, collecting paintings by European masters such as Monet and Degas and having his palace rebuilt as a replica of the French royal palace at Versailles, Kawamura's home was a simple Japanese wooden house. Floors were made of reed mats called *tatami*, and thin pallets were used for sleeping. Illustrated paper screens cordoned off sections of rooms, and sliding panels separated rooms. There was a prayer and meditation room and several miniature gardens.

Hirohito's younger brother, Yasuhito (the future Prince Chichibu), soon joined him with the Kawamura family. The count took the responsibility of raising the future emperor very seriously and set three goals for the molding of his character: First, to teach him to fear nothing and also treat his elders with respect; second, to train him to endure hardships and difficulties; third, to guide him to be neither selfish nor willful. In 1904 the count passed away. The two princes remained with his family for another year, until 1905, and then returned to the imperial court.

Hirohito at age three, while he was still under the foster care of Count Kawamura Sumiyoshi, who had assisted in the development of the Japanese navy. It was a tradition for royal infants to spend their earliest years with a trusted noble family.

Young Hirohito in the uniform of the *Gakushuin*, or Peers' School, where children of the royal family and the aristocracy were educated. The headmaster, Nogi Maresuke, taught Hirohito *bushido*, the code of values of Japan's warrior class, the *samurai*.

During Hirohito's early years, Japan's growing confidence was displayed in the form of an increasingly active, aggressive foreign policy. Since 1853 the Japanese had established a modern army and navy, built a new railroad system, and made great industrial advances, but Japan's second-class status in regard to the Western powers remained unchanged. Unequal trade agreements with the West were still in existence. Particularly galling to the Japanese were the provisions in the treaties calling for *extraterritoriality*, which meant that a Russian citizen, for example, who committed a crime on Japanese soil could not be tried in Japanese courts under Japanese law but had to be handed over to the Russians for trial. The extraterritoriality provisions said to the Japanese that the Western nations considered Japan and Japanese ways inferior to their own.

Hirohito at 13. Some people suggested that because of his frail physique, poor eyesight, and withdrawn personality Hirohito was unsuited to rule. They advocated that he be bypassed as crown prince in favor of his more robust younger brother Yasuhito, the future Prince Chichibu.

In 1894–95 Japan, which had been gradually expanding its influence in the nation of Korea, defeated Chinese troops there who were aiding the Korean monarch in trying to suppress a Japanese-sponsored rebellion. By virtue of the peace treaty ending the war, Japan received valuable territories — the most valuable being the Liaotung Peninsula in Manchuria — and effective control over Korea, but Russia, France, and Germany combined to "persuade" Japan to relinquish its new possessions. Japan had no real choice. Despite its newfound strength, Japan was not ready to challenge the combined forces of three European powers. Hirohito's grandfather, Emperor Meiji, told his people that they "must bear the unbearable" — words his grandson would echo years later — and accept the Triple Intervention.

Nine years later the intervention still rankled, particularly as Britain, France, Germany, the United States, and Russia continued to claim Asian territories for themselves. The Russian intercession was perhaps the greatest affront to Japan, as Russia's location made it Japan's most immediate rival in Asia. Japan still coveted Manchuria and its natural resources, which the Russians had been busy developing, and was irked by Russia's challenge to its interests in Korea. In February 1904 the Japanese navy attacked Russian ships off Port Arthur (now

Lüshun) in Manchuria, launching the Russo-Japanese War. It lasted for 18 months, and to the surprise of much of the world, Japan defeated the Russians decisively, on land and at sea. In little more than 50 years Japan had grown from a nation unable to defend itself to one capable of defeating the largest nation on earth. In the treaty that ended the war (the Treaty of Portsmouth) Japan won territorial concessions in Manchuria and elsewhere and recognition of its interests in Korea, which Japan annexed in 1910.

State concerns were far from Hirohito's mind in 1905. At the imperial court, where it was an ancient custom to provide separate living quarters for each member of the imperial family, Hirohito and Yasuhito each had a small palace. They spent a great deal of time together in the gardens and open areas of the imperial grounds with their governess and any number of adult playmates — palace chamberlains or ladies-in-waiting. They saw their parents much less frequently; their mother once or twice a week, their father once a month. Hirohito's favorite game was *shippo tori* (catching tails), in which one player

Hirohito as a young man. In addition to being schooled in bushido, Hirohito learned military tactics and history in preparation for the day when, as emperor, he would serve as commander in chief of the Japanese armed forces.

A rare photograph of Taisho and Hirohito together. Taisho saw Hirohito only about once a month when the boy was young.

would tie a white handkerchief to the back of his belt and the others would try to grab this "tail." Kanroji Osanaga, the emperor's grand chamberlain, recalled that the little prince "always played strictly according to the rules, never employing any of the little tricks that were possible in this game."

In 1908 Hirohito was enrolled in the *Gakushuin*, or Peers' School, where his brothers (he now had a second, Nobuhito, the future Prince Takamatsu) and the children of Japan's aristocracy were educated in geography, science, English, handwriting and drawing (the Japanese writing system is extremely complicated, consisting of thousands of pictographic characters), singing, manual training, and gymnastics. The Gakushuin's headmaster was General Nogi Maresuke, the hero of the siege of Port Arthur during Japan's war with Russia. Nogi had a profound effect on Hirohito. He was an adherent of *bushido*, the code of the warrior class — the *samurai*. Traditionally, the samurai had been the feudal retainers of Japan's landowning nobility. Bushido called for a total disdain for commercial concerns. The samurai were forbidden to handle money and were completely dependent on their masters for food, clothing, and their livelihood. The ancient castes — warrior, artisan, peasant, and merchant — were officially abolished in 1876, but bushido was cultivated among the armed forces as a way of instilling courage and discipline. Most important among bushido's values was loyalty, particularly to one's feudal lord. A samurai whose lord died became a *ronin*, or masterless warrior, although some samurai, out of loyalty to their master, committed seppuko, or *hara-kiri* — ritual suicide through disembowelment. Seppuko was also used to atone for mistakes or crimes and to maintain honor in the face of disgrace or defeat.

Nogi immediately set strict guidelines for the young prince's training. Primary consideration was to be given to health. Hirohito was not to be treated specially; punishment for misbehavior was not to be moderated. The habit of diligence was to be instilled. The prince was to be reared simply and plainly, and attention was to be given to preparation for future military duties. Hirohito's teachers were all former members of the army or navy, for his main public function would be that of *daigensui*, commander in chief of the armed forces.

A Japanese artist's portrayal of the Sino-Japanese War. Eager to acquire its own empire, Japan defeated China in 1894—95 and gained Korea and part of Manchuria; but Russia, France, and Germany forced Japan to part with its territory in Manchuria.

The victory procession in Tokyo for the returning Admiral Togo Heihachiro, one of the heroes of the Russo-Japanese War. In 1904 Japan's interest in Manchuria brought it to war with Russia, which also claimed privileges in the region. Japan's stunning victory announced to the world that it had become a major power.

Special attention was paid to Hirohito's physical education. The prince had inherited a minor muscular disorder that ran in the royal family and reduced his gait to a stooped shuffle, and his poor vision increased the impression of physical frailty. Bushido stressed courage and a stoic indifference to physical discomfort and pain. As a boy Nogi had been made to kneel naked in the snow while his father poured freezing water over him, and later he lost an eye while fencing and was crippled in battle. Under Nogi's tutelage Hirohito was made to stand under an ice-cold waterfall until he could do so without shivering.

The prince was very bright, even a bit precocious, but he had trouble with those subjects that required manual dexterity and was also poor at calisthenics and sports. Kanroji, in diaries he published after serving the imperial family for 70 years, notes that Hirohito managed to develop into an excellent swimmer through willpower and determination. "No matter how long he took or what the results might be," says Kanroji of the young prince, "he never quit halfway, but always persevered to the end." The same persistence was applied to mastering horseback riding, golf, and tennis.

At the Peers' School Hirohito first came to understand the duties and responsibilities that fell upon him as the likely heir to the Japanese throne. Despite the attempts to ensure that he was not spoiled or pampered, Hirohito could not help but be aware that his royal birth made him special. He began to develop a certain reserve with other people. Nogi encouraged Hirohito to be aware and proud of his royal ancestry. Among the rules of behavior he prescribed for Hirohito was one encouraging him to "inquire of your parents about your ancestors, your crest and lineage, and keep them well in mind." It was at the Peers' School that Hirohito first showed an interest in biology, which was to be a lifetime love, and exhibited a proficiency at writing *tanka*, a traditional Japanese poetic form.

Japanese soldiers fire from trenches during the Russo-Japanese War. The high casualty figures from the land battles of the war foretold the great human cost of World War I, which would begin 10 years later.

The samurai were pre-Meiji Japan's warrior caste. Above all, they prized honor, courage, and loyalty to their master. After the abolition of the ancient castes in 1876, the samurai's code was instilled in the armed forces, with the emperor the object of his soldiers' loyalty.

In the summer of 1912 Emperor Meiji became critically ill. Hirohito returned from the royal villa at Hayama, where he had been enthusiastically collecting marine specimens for scientific study. Meiji's death on July 29 brought to an end a remarkable reign that had witnessed the transformation of Japan into a world power.

Meiji came to the throne in 1867, when he was just 15 years old. His given name was Mutsuhito, but Japanese emperors traditionally select a name to characterize their reign, and Mutsuhito called himself Meiji, which means enlightened rule.

Meiji became emperor 14 years after Matthew Perry had reopened Japan to the West. The influx of Western traders and new technology and ideas that followed the arrival of the black ships accelerated change within Japan. In 1600 Tokugawa Ieyasu and his allies defeated rival lords at the Battle of Sekigahara, bringing to an end more than 100 years of civil war. Ieyasu's consolidation of power as the *shogun* (military governor) of Japan completed a process whereby the emperors virtually ceded all governmental and military authority to the shoguns. For the next 250 years the Tokugawa shoguns and their advisers ruled Japan from Tokyo, then called Edo, while the emperors presided from the ancient capital of Kyoto. It was the Tokugawas who enacted the policy of sakoku, but the coming of the black ships revealed how weak Japan had grown under their rule.

Under the Tokugawas there had always been those who advocated the restoration of the emperor's power, chiefly from among the clans defeated at Sekigahara and effectively kept from power by the Tokugawas since then. Japan's inability to repel the Westerners in the 1850s gave impetus to the movement, providing evidence that the shoguns had failed in their responsibility to protect the nation. "Revere the emperor; expel the barbarians [foreigners]!" became the battle cry of the restorationists. Civil war, assassinations, and attacks on foreign settlements marked the early 1860s, with the restorationists gradually growing in power. Shortly after Mutsuhito took the throne in 1867, he issued an imperial rescript announcing the restoration of direct imperial rule. Tokugawa forces were

As a young man Hirohito was a diligent but skeptical student. He frustrated his teachers by deriding the myths of Japan's divine origins as scientifically unsound and by questioning the blind patriotism of his military tutors. He developed an interest in marine biology that became his life's passion.

Buddhism came to Japan from China in the 6th century A.D. and has since coexisted with Shinto, Japan's indigenous religion. Most Japanese practice both. Shinto is concerned primarily with the practice of detailed rites, and scholars argue that Buddhism provided Japanese religion with its ethical content.

defeated by imperial troops, and Meiji moved the imperial capital to Edo, which was renamed Tokyo.

The Meiji Restoration was a mixture of the traditional and the new. Although theoretically possessing absolute power, the emperor was still beholden to tradition and ruled as much through suggestion and influence as decree or fiat. Meiji's reign was blessed by an extremely able group of advisers who had been excluded from power under the Tokugawas and were eager to direct Japan on a new course.

Despite the rhetoric about expelling the foreigners, Meiji and his advisers determined that the quickest way for Japan to strengthen itself was to adopt Western ways. The military was organized along Western lines, railroads and industries were built with the help of Western advisers, and Western-style banks and financial institutions were established. Imperial edicts abolished the old feudal castes. Western novels, music, art, and clothing became popular. Soon Japan was ready to emulate the Western nations — many of whom had colonial possessions in Africa, Asia, South and Central America, and the Middle East — by establishing its own empire, beginning with Korea and Manchuria.

At the same time the Japanese heritage was emphasized. Shinto, which had been eclipsed by Buddhism but had long been associated with the restorationists, enjoyed a resurgence and was installed as the state religion. Education was made mandatory, and State Shinto, emphasizing the divine origins of the imperial line, was taught. In the armed services, which were now open to all Japanese, not just members of the samurai caste (although virtually all officers were samurais or descendants of members of that caste), bushido was instilled, with the emperor as the focus of the code of loyalty.

The Meiji Constitution was the perfect example of the restoration's blend of the traditional and the new. Based on the German constitution, it was bestowed as a gift from Meiji to his people in 1889. The Meiji Constitution established a representative

Shinto priests at the Meiji Temple. Shinto incorporated worship of Japan's native gods and ancestor veneration. It deemed the emperor to be of divine descent and regarded him as the religion's high priest.

assembly, the Diet, which consisted of two chambers — the House of Peers, consisting of members of the nobility, and a House of Representatives. Membership in the House of Peers was essentially hereditary, although some members were appointed by the emperor. The House of Representatives was an elected body, but less than one percent of the population was eligible to vote. Real power continued to rest with the emperor's advisers, in the form of the privy council and a cabinet, which was presided over by a prime minister, chosen by the emperor in consultation with his advisers. The first sentence of the constitution stated that "Japan shall be reigned over and governed by a line of emperors unbroken for ages eternal."

With Meiji's death, Yoshihito took the throne. He took the reign name Taisho, which means great righteousness, but he possessed few of his father's leadership qualities. A great admirer of the Germans, he liked nothing better than to dress up in a German military uniform and often struck out at those around him with a riding crop. Like his father, he greatly enjoyed the company of the palace concubines (Taisho himself was Meiji's son by one of the concubines), but he displayed none of his father's subtlety in exercising power.

Taisho's reign began with a political crisis brought about by the collapse of the government of Prime Minister Saionji Kimmochi. Two of the cabinet posts — the war and defense ministries — were in Japan's constitutional government customarily filled by military officers, who gained Taisho's support for increased military spending, ostensibly to defend, if not expand, Japan's new empire. Military spending was leading Japan toward an economic crisis, and Saionji's opposition caused his government to fall. The emperor's appointment of a pro-military prime minister resulted in rioting — it was believed that the emperor was riding roughshod over the desires of the cabinet and the Diet, and the emperor was not expected to be visible — and the eventual resignation of the new prime minister, General Katsura Taro, in favor of a more frugal cabinet.

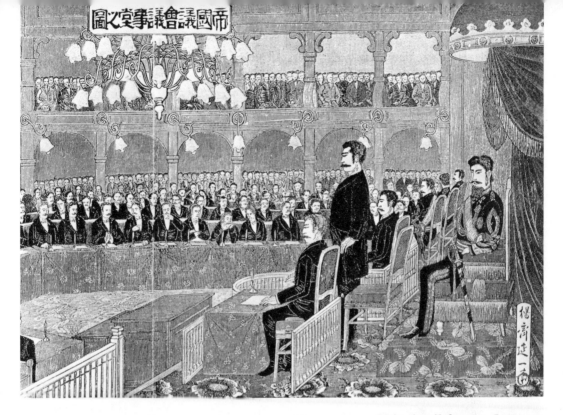

It was customary that as the emperor's eldest son Hirohito would be named crown prince, but it was possible that because of his slight physical infirmities he could be bypassed. Some courtiers and nobles, Nogi among them, recommended that Prince Chichibu, Hirohito's more dashing and athletic brother, be named heir to the throne, but Taisho held out for Hirohito. On September 9, 1912, he was officially proclaimed heir.

Three days later he was visited by Nogi, who advised him to take his new responsibilities with grave seriousness. Nogi then urged Chichibu and Takamatsu to help their brother. Upon his return home, Nogi and his wife committed seppuku. It was said that he had wished to commit seppuku after the Russo-Japanese War in atonement for the nearly 60,000 Japanese — including his two sons — killed under his command at Port Arthur, but had been directly forbidden to do so by Meiji. With the emperor's death, Nogi was free to follow his master to Shinto's spirit world. He left behind a note lamenting the selfishness of the young Japanese and exhorting all Japanese to adhere to the values of bushido.

This detail from a Japanese engraving shows the convening of the first session of the Diet in 1890. The Diet was established by the Meiji constitution of 1889, which was largely the work of the conservative statesman Ito Hirobumi. The constitution was based on the German model and gave the Diet only limited power.

3

Crown Prince in an Ambitious Era

The *Togu-gogakumonjo*, or Imperial Palace School, was established in 1914 to continue Hirohito's education. Admiral Togo Shigenori, hero of the final, decisive Battle of Tsushima Strait in the Russo-Japanese War, was appointed headmaster. There was little rapport between the two, and Togo generally left Hirohito's education in the hands of his tutors. Hirohito had begun to grow disillusioned with the blind patriotism espoused by the military and the vainglorious sacrifices it demanded, such as the suicide of Nogi. The crown prince, now a lieutenant in the army and ensign in the navy, did develop an interest in military tactics and strategy.

The curriculum at the new school was extremely rigorous. Hirohito received lessons in ethics, history, mathematics, geography, science, Japanese and Chinese literature, natural history, physical science, French, law and economy, and the history of fine arts. Although a good student with an outstanding memory, Hirohito had some difficulties

[Hirohito] grew up in a peculiarly insular world which had developed for centuries in isolation from other nations. Anthropologists, poets, priests, and diplomats, each in their own field, have found, on study, that the Japanese world contains a logic and a beauty of its own.
—SIR WILLIAM FLOOD WEBB
Chief Justice of the Allied trials of Japan's major war criminals

Hirohito astride his famous white charger, which became his trademark.

keeping up with his studies, a problem compounded by the dullness of his lecturers and his growing skepticism. His interest in biology was leading Hirohito to develop an increasingly scientific and rational turn of mind, and he repeatedly disagreed with lecturers who stressed the divine origins of the royal family, observing that the tales were biologically impossible. Word of the prince's doubts reached the *genro*, the elder statesmen or advisers who had been instrumental in establishing the constitution and governing Japan since. Prince Saionji Kimmochi was dispatched to speak with the prince and sought to convince him that although it was not necessary for Hirohito to believe in the divine origins, the Japanese people needed to believe in the myth. It was part of the national essence. It was in the greater interests of the Japanese nation, which it was the emperor's duty to protect, that the emperor be revered as divine, and so long as there were no public disavowals by the prince, he could entertain his private doubts. The skeptical prince was swayed by Saionji's arguments.

Togo Heihachiro (far left) was Japan's foremost military hero and was made headmaster of the special school created for Hirohito in 1914; but the suicide of Hirohito's earlier mentor, Nogi Maresuke, left the crown prince with a distrust of militarism, and there was little empathy between Togo and his royal pupil.

The prince's frail constitution and poor eyesight continued to be a worry. Hamao Arata, the grand master of the crown prince's household, attempted to assume a fatherly position by nagging Hirohito about his posture and expressing worries about his nearsightedness. It simply would not do, he insisted, for the future emperor of Japan to wear spectacles. He had heard that myopia could be improved by looking frequently at distant objects, so he ordered the trees on the south side of the prince's palace removed so that the coast of Shinagawa could be seen. When Hirohito's vision worsened from gazing at the coast, the therapy was abandoned. Spectacles were ordered, as was a back brace, in the hope that his posture might be made more princely.

There were some teachers whom Hirohito enjoyed. Among them was Sugiura Jugo, his ethics tutor, who stressed the inherent superiority of the Japanese and their way of life but cautioned that both England and Russia were at the moment stronger than Japan. Hirohito's favorite was his natural history teacher, Hattori Hirotaro, who was to become a lifelong friend. Hattori encouraged the prince's interest in biology, and the two spent many hours hiking in the hills surrounding the imperial villa. Hattori trained Hirohito to observe the smallest details in nature and fostered the prince's interest in marine biology. When the prince complained that the large retinue of bodyguards

Crown Prince Hirohito captured in a rare informal moment. He felt constrained by the restrictions placed on him by his position and duties and envied the European monarchs for the comparative freedom with which they interacted with their subjects.

By 1921 Taisho was incapable of fulfilling his responsibilities as emperor, and Hirohito (left, on horseback) was made prince regent. Uncertain of his authority, he relied on the counsel of his advisers, particularly the *genro* (elder statesman) Saionji Kimmochi.

and courtiers that was obligated to accompany him on his walks ruined his appreciation of nature, Hattari suggested they collect aquatic specimens. Hirohito and Hattari would sail onto Sagami Bay in a small boat, accompanied only by two pearl divers, who would obtain specimens for study by the prince and his teacher. Hirohito soon became an accomplished diver himself, and a small laboratory was built in his palace so that he could study the specimens he collected.

In 1914 World War I broke out in Europe and the Middle East, pitting the Allies (Great Britain, France, Italy, Russia, and later the United States) against the Central Powers (Germany, Austria-Hungary, and Turkey). Emperor Taisho was himself pro-German, but his advisers, led by Foreign Minister Kato Takaaki, aligned Japan with the Allies, all the while casting a covetous eye on Germany's colonial possessions in China.

China was the most populous nation in the world, but its poverty and the weakness of its Qing (or Manchu) dynasty emperors had left it easy prey for foreign exploitation. In the 19th century the European nations forced on China a series of unequal treaties, thereby gaining favorable trade arrangements and establishing spheres of influence and concessions, which were areas within China that the foreign powers essentially governed. With Germany occupied with its war in Europe, Japan moved on the German-leased city of Tsingtao, on China's Shantung Peninsula, and after a long seige gained control of the city and the peninsula.

Emboldened by his success, Kato then pressed upon the Chinese government what became known as the 21 Demands, which ordered China to transfer all German rights to Japan, extend Japan's rights in Manchuria, employ Japanese political and military advisers, allow Japanese police to patrol certain Chinese cities, buy half of its military supplies from Japan, allow the Japanese to construct a network of railroads, and go to Japan for all loans, in collateral for which China would relinquish control of its iron industry.

The 21 Demands revealed the extent of Japan's imperial ambitions. Although some of the more noxious provisions (from the Chinese point of view) were eliminated by the victorious Allies at the Paris Peace Conference, where the Treaty of Versailles was negotiated, the 21 Demands changed world opinion of the Japanese. Whereas Japan's reputation had been enhanced by its unexpected victory over Russia — tiny Japan had defeated mighty Russia — the Western nations deplored what they viewed as Japan's bullying of defenseless China. Although the Western reaction was no doubt based on economic self-interest, in that the Western nations had no desire for a powerful rival to their own commercial and political concerns in China and elsewhere, Asian nations were also apprehensive about the growing strength of Japan, which had taken Korea and now apparently wished to do the same to China.

The most important consequence of the 21 Demands was that it set Japan on a collision course with the United States, which had a special interest in China. Many Chinese had immigrated to the United States, and many U.S. missionaries were active in China. There had recently been a revolution in China in which the Qing dynasty had been overthrown, and the revolution's leader, Sun Yat-sen, hoped to establish a republican government. Sun had visited the United States and received much of his funding from the Chinese expatriate community

Sun Yat-sen led the revolution that overthrew China's Qing dynasty in 1912. Japan pressed upon the weak government that followed the Twenty-one Demands, the series of claims that were a severe affront to Chinese sovereignty and first brought Japan into conflict with the United States.

Hirohito's selection of Princess Nagako (shown here as a young girl) as his fiancée aroused controversy. Meiji and Taisho had both allowed their advisers to choose their brides for them, and Count Yamagata Aritomo, an influential noble, directed a campaign against Hirohito's engagement.

there, and China's experiment with republicanism was viewed very favorably in the U.S. press. Over the years the United States government would take an increasingly active role in the attempt by the Chinese republicans to establish a central government, a goal at odds with the Japanese desire for territorial expansion there.

The Treaty of Versailles in 1921 left the Japanese unsatisfied. Although proud to sit with the United States, France, Great Britain, and Italy as victors, Japan was not happy at being compelled to return the Shantung Peninsula. The Japanese saw a certain duplicity in the Western nations, which sought to restrain Japan's attempts at empire building while rewarding themselves more colonial possessions in the Middle East and Africa from the dispersed empires of the defeated nations. Japanese suspicions that the West regarded them as inferior were not eased when the Paris delegates refused to pass a resolution declaring racial equality among nations.

After the turmoil that accompanied the military-spending affair, Taisho stopped playing an active role in the government. He suffered a series of cerebral blood clots that further impaired his judgment. While reviewing troops he sometimes fell from his horse. On one occasion he whipped one of the soldiers for no reason. He was gradually eased into the background by his advisers. As Taisho declined, it was thought that Hirohito should become more visible to the public. In 1916 a picture of him in his navy uniform appeared in the newspapers. An accompanying article reported that he was five foot six (tall by Japanese standards) and enjoyed tennis, and gave the text of his favorite poem:

> The light of the Sun
> And Moon
> Withholds no favors;
> They shine equally
> Upon all.

With Taisho's health deteriorating, it was important that a secure line of succession be assured, so attention was turned to Hirohito's marriage. The advisers, particularly Count Yamagata Aritomo, the architect of the new Japanese army under Meiji and the last survivor of the great genro from that period, expected that Hirohito would follow custom and marry the bride they selected. The great Meiji had done so, and Taisho married his wife sight unseen. To have the future empress selected from one's family could only increase one's prestige and influence. The great noble clans that had dominated Japanese history still provided most of Japan's military and political leaders. The two greatest western clans — the Satsumas and Choshus — who had been largely excluded from power after the Battle of Sekigahara but had their influence restored after backing Meiji in the restoration struggle, dominated the modern Japanese military, with men from the Choshu effectively controlling the army and the Satsumas running the navy.

Yamagata was a Choshu. He had several candidates for the imperial marriage in mind, but Hirohito had his own ideas. Aided by his mother, Empress Sadako, who arranged for several potential brides to come to a tea ceremony at the palace, which Hirohito watched from a hiding place behind a screened panel, Hirohito made his own choice. On February 4, 1918, the palace announced Hirohito's marriage to Princess Nagako, the 15-year-old daughter of Kuni Kuniyoshi. Hirohito knew Nagako slightly; the young couple would not get to know one another much better before their engagement. They met only nine times over the six years of their engagement, never alone.

Yamagata was unhappy with the match. Nagako's mother was a Satsuma, and the betrothal promised that clan increased contacts and influence at court. He tried to force an end to the match by introducing evidence that Nagako's branch of the family was afflicted by color blindness, which allegedly indicated a hereditary weakness in the future crown princess that could not be permitted to weaken the imperial bloodlines. But Kuni, the empress, and Sugiura Jugo, the crown prince's ethics teacher, supported the match, with Kuni threatening that he and his daughter would commit seppuku if the

> *She had, in fact, many of the qualities of her future mother-in-law, the Empress—strength of character, solid good sense and instinctive shrewdness—plus a bubbling sense of humor which did not allow her to take even her setbacks too seriously for too long.*
> —LEONARD MOSLEY
> author, describing Nagako,
> Hirohito's wife

In 1921 Hirohito became the first Japanese crown prince to leave the home islands when he visited several European countries. His trip to England was a particular success, and he greatly enjoyed his informal discussions with Edward, Prince of Wales (right), the future King Edward VIII.

betrothal were broken. Hirohito, in his mild-mannered but firm way, refused to consider a new bride, replying only, "I prefer Nagako," when asked about the controversy. Ultimately, Yamagata capitulated.

Having just completed seven arduous years of study at the Togu-gogakumonjo, Hirohito embarked on a grand tour of Europe. His primary destination was England, where he was to solidify Japan's relations with Great Britain, which had been formalized by a treaty of alliance that was still in effect. On the night of March 3, 1921, the battleship *Katori* anchored near Hayama, and the crown prince, in his new admiral's uniform, came on deck to bow in the direction of his parents' villa. Then the vessel, joined by a fleet of destroyers, pushed off toward Hong Kong. It was the first time in Japanese history that the crown prince had traveled abroad.

Hirohito prepared for his arrival on the Continent by studying French and English and reading French and British history. He relaxed by swimming or playing deck golf. The prince's party stopped in Cairo, in Malta — where he attended theater for the first time in his life — and in Gibraltar before arriving in London. It was not the best time for a visit; the war's end had prompted widespread economic disequilibrium, and Britain was still suffering from strikes, work stoppages, and high unemployment, but the crown prince's visit was an enormous success. He attended numerous banquets, visited museums, and stayed at the centuries-old Scottish castle of the duke of Atholl, where he was taken hunting and fishing. The British were captivated by his modest demeanor, his poise and self-assurance, his evident intelligence, and his knowledge of British life and history. Most of all, they were charmed by Hirohito's obvious enjoyment of his stay, for the crown prince was utterly taken with what he saw as the complete ease and informality of British life. He greatly envied the freedom of movement of the British monarch, George V, and his son and heir to the throne, Edward, prince of Wales. The British royal family was able to attend the theater, go to the racetrack, and dine at a restaurant, and Hirohito compared the seeming lack of barriers between the British royal family and their subjects with his own more cloistered existence.

Cheering throngs gathered at Tokyo's railroad station to greet Hirohito upon his return to Japan from Europe in September 1921. The crown prince's solemnity, dignity, intelligence, and curiosity had earned him a favorable press in the nations he visited.

From London, Hirohito went on to visit France, Belgium, the Netherlands, and Italy and was similarly well received. News of his successes preceded his journey home, and he was greeted on arrival in Tokyo on September 3 by a large, enthusiastic crowd. He later said that his European trip had been the happiest, most carefree time of his life. Taisho had grown more ill, and after his return Hirohito was made prince regent and assumed the duties of the emperor. Not all of the genro and advisers were pleased with this development, for Taisho's illness had left them virtually free to govern as they wished, and Hirohito had shown signs of an independent turn of mind. Saionji, who had been elevated to the ranks of the genro, feared that Hirohito had developed dangerous republican leanings while in England and worried that the new regent intended to move Japan toward a true constitutional monarchism.

With Taisho all but abdicating his responsibilities, Japan's aggressive foreign policy had continued unchecked. In 1918 the Japanese army had invaded Siberia, although Japan ultimately received no territory from its incursion. When the economic boom that had accompanied World War I subsided in the early 1920s, widespread unemployment and labor unrest resulted. There had been riots over the high cost of rice even before the end of the war, and prices continued to rise. Popular opinion turned against the military and the military spending that was compounding Japan's economic problems, but there were few mechanisms whereby public opinion could make itself felt. The advisers and genro had little interest in making Japan more democratic, as the current system allowed them to all but rule Japan by identifying themselves with the wishes of the emperor at the same time that the loyalty of the populace to the emperor was assured. The adoption of a cabinet government and a parliamentary system at about the time the Meiji Constitution was proclaimed seemed to promise a move toward democracy, but the Diet was elected by only a small percentage of the population. Those eligible to vote were almost invariably large landowners or members of the upper classes, most of whom were very conservative. The prime minister and the members of the cabinet did not have to be members of the Diet, and the cabinet was traditionally composed of members of the prominent Japanese families and rarely reflected the party representation in the Diet. The genro and other influential and well-connected Japanese often did not possess official government positions but wielded as much power in their capacity as advisers as those who did. Furthermore, the tradition that only military officers could fill the cabinet positions of war minister, navy minister, and army minister and the ability of the army and navy chiefs of staff to veto certain cabinet measures ensured that the military's point of view was always strongly represented. It also made possible the type of strong-arm tactics used by the military in the spending crisis that accompanied Taisho's accession to the throne. If the military ministers opposed cabinet policy, they simply resigned. Out of clan (the military ministers were usually Satsumas or Choshus), class, and service loyalty, other officers would refuse to serve as minister, and the government would collapse. The government also controlled public opinion through the judicious use of the secret police, and a Japanese man or woman could be arrested merely for "dangerous thoughts."

Hirohito visits a devastated section of Tokyo after the September 1923 earthquake. The prince regent's tours through the afflicted areas did much to restore public confidence, but in the immediate aftermath of the disaster Hirohito failed to allay the panic that resulted in the massacre of many Koreans living in Tokyo.

The premiership of Hara Takashi offered some hope for change. Hara became prime minister in 1918. Known as the "Great Commoner," he was only the third prime minister since the Meiji Constitution who was not a Satsuma or a Choshu, and he was known to favor increased suffrage and democratic privileges. Hara's government could make some claim to represent popular opinion — all of his cabinet members but three were members of the majority party in the Diet — but in 1921 he was assassinated by a right-wing activist. Hara's alleged crime was "defiling the Constitution" by making himself temporary naval minister (no civilian was supposed to serve in that post) while the minister was in Washington, D.C., at a diplomatic conference, but his real sin was his support for liberalization. The claim that he was acting to protect the constitution won Hara's assassin public sympathy, and he received a light sentence of only 12 years in jail.

On September 1, 1923, a powerful earthquake rocked Japan. Its epicenter was near Tokyo and Yokohama, and the cities were nearly destroyed. The quake struck near noon, when most Japanese were preparing their midday meal on charcoal braziers. It was not long before the overturned braziers ignited the remains of the collapsed wooden houses, and flames rushed through the cities. Over three-quarters of Yokohama and one-half of Tokyo were destroyed, and numerous smaller villages and towns were equally hard hit. One hundred and forty thousand Japanese were killed.

The earthquake disrupted communications and left Yokohama, Tokyo, and the surrounding areas isolated. Thousands of Japanese were left homeless. Rumors of gangs of Korean looters and the imminent arrival of a Korean army spread. (The Koreans were the objects of considerable racial prejudice in Japan. The Koreans and the Japanese had a tradition of animosity toward one another, fueled by their nations' troubled relations. Japan had annexed Korea in 1910, and many Koreans migrated to Japan, where they were discriminated against and found it difficult to obtain work. They were con-

Hirohito and Nagako on their wedding day, January 26, 1924. After the wedding the Japanese people eagerly awaited the announcement that Nagako was pregnant, but the royal couple's first child was a girl and as such was not an heir to the throne.

sequently among the poorest classes in Japan and were believed by the Japanese to be responsible for much of the nation's crime.) Decisive action was needed to stem the incipient hysteria, but the government remained silent. Hirohito remained at the palace, waiting for someone to advise him, but Saionji was away from Tokyo and no direction was forthcoming. Mobs of angry Japanese, eager to find a scapegoat for the disaster, roamed the streets searching for Koreans, thousands of whom were beaten, tortured, or summarily executed.

Hirohito emerged from the palace days later and rode through the city on horseback, surveying the damage. His presence assured his people that the crisis was under control, but by that point the riots had already run their course. The emperor announced that he was postponing his wedding because it was not suitable to celebrate in such times and donated the equivalent of $2.5 million from his own funds for emergency relief. Although traditional Japanese belief held that earthquakes were caused by the movements of a giant catfish that lived on the ocean bottom beneath the Japanese islands and stirred only when Amaterasu was displeased with the emperor, the cheering throngs that greeted Hirohito's passage through Tokyo attested to his continued popularity.

Fourteen weeks after the earthquake, on December 27, 1923, Hirohito was shot at while riding in the imperial limousine to a special session of the Diet on the reconstruction of Tokyo. The shot narrowly missed Hirohito; it was fired by Namba Daisuke, a young labor activist. Despite intense police interrogation aimed at uncovering his accomplices, the would-be assassin steadfastly maintained that he had acted alone, in protest of the mass arrests by the secret police of socialists, labor union organizers, and other dissidents in the chaotic days that followed the great earthquake. Namba was executed the following November. The assassination attempt benefited the more conservative elements in the Japanese government, who used it to illustrate the dangers of liberalization and to convince Hirohito to keep a lower profile. He appeared in public much less frequently thereafter.

The failed assassination did not further delay Hirohito's marriage. For six years Nagako had waited, in near seclusion, as she was tutored in the rigorous protocol and etiquette required of the Japanese empress. During that time she had met with her fiancé only nine times. He had not written her while abroad and sent her no messages while the controversy over her suitability raged. Finally, on January 26, 1924, the wedding took place. The *New York Times* described the long-awaited event: "With all the picturesque but subdued Shinto setting, before the ancestral shrine within the moated Palace of Emperors, and with the ancient ceremonial and costumes, Princess Nagako today became the bride of Crown Prince Hirohito, Prince Regent of Japan." There were 700 guests; a nationwide holiday was declared for the rest of the month.

Following a quiet honeymoon in Okinajima, the imperial couple returned to Tokyo and just as quietly began married life behind the great gates of the imperial palace. Isolated from the noise and congestion of Tokyo, the palace contained more than 200 acres of woods and gardens, pavilions, pools, greenhouses, stables, a nine-hole golf course, an administration building, a library, and many residential palaces. Hirohito's biological laboratory and its offices, a nursery, and over a thousand square yards of fields were also part of this world. In the main palace, the rooms had been decorated for the crown prince and princess in an elegant European style, with stained-glass windows, golden chandeliers, oil paintings, marble fireplaces, teak bookshelves, and plush carpeting.

The absence of an immediate announcement of Nagako's pregnancy caused much discussion, as the production of a royal heir was a subject of national concern. Among the rumors spread concerning the royal couple was one stating that Nagako had been cursed by Yamagata after the marriage controversy. News in the spring of 1925 that Nagako was expecting temporarily brought an end to such speculations. A daughter, Terunomiya, was born to Hirohito and Nagako on December 6, 1925, but her birth only rekindled controversy, as only a male child could inherit the throne.

Taisho died a little more than a year after the birth of Hirohito and Nagako's child. Although the official enthronement would take place later, Hirohito became emperor immediately upon his father's death. On December 28, two days after ascending to the throne, he issued his first imperial rescript, which he wrote himself: "With Our limited gifts, We are mindful of the difficulty of proving Ourselves equal to the great task which has devolved upon Us. The world is now in a process of evolution. A new chapter is being opened in the history of human civilization. This nation's settled policy always stands for progress and improvement. Simplicity instead of vain display, originality instead of blind imitation, progress in view of this period of evolution, improvement to keep pace with the advancement of civilization, national harmony in purpose and action, beneficence to all classes of people, and friendship to all the nations of the earth: these are the cardinal aims to which Our most profound and abiding solicitude is directed."

On the same day it was announced that he would call his reign *Showa*, or enlightened peace.

4

The Rise of the Militarists

Hirohito's official enthronement took place in the ancient imperial capital of Kyoto in November 1928. It was an extremely lavish ceremony, full of pomp and Shinto ritual. On the first day Hirohito and his empress prayed to Amaterasu and were then officially enthroned. The second day was spent on bathing and purification rituals and prayer services. The last day was the *Daijosai*, or Thanksgiving Festival. The emperor, alone in two specially constructed sacred huts, spent the day in prayer, making offerings to the goddess of the food ritual. He emerged at dawn, confirmed in ancient ceremony as the 124th in the unbroken line of Japanese emperors.

There were reasons for optimism as Hirohito began his reign. Party government had made inroads at the expense of military domination of the government. Between 1922 and 1927 military spending was trimmed from 42 percent of the national budget to 28 percent, and four entire army divisions

Is it possible for any mortal to forget an experience like this? Will not the remembrance of devotions so unique follow him through life? This is ancestor worship pure and simple, fidelity to the past pledged to the duties of the present and the services of the future.
—*Times* of London correspondent describing Hirohito's enthronement

Although Hirohito became emperor upon the death of Taisho in December 1926, his official enthronement did not take place until November 1928. He is shown here in his ceremonial garb on the first day of the ritual.

were eliminated. The military had become so unpopular in some areas that soldiers stopped wearing their uniforms while off duty. The right to vote was extended, so that by 1925 all male subjects over the age of 25 were eligible to cast a ballot. This amounted to 20 percent of the population. In the initial election after the proclamation of the Meiji Constitution, held in 1890, less than one percent of the population had been eligible to vote.

But in 1927 Japan suffered an economic depression that caused the virtual collapse of many sections of the economy. In 1927 alone, 36 banks were forced to close. Jobs were lost, and workers' real wages plummeted. Japan took tentative steps toward recovery, but by 1930 the entire world economy had collapsed, further aggravating the situation in Japan. By 1931 3 million Japanese were without work. Hardest hit were Japanese farmers, particularly in northern Japan, where the depression and the failure of the rice crop led to famine and starvation. Small businessmen also suffered. Many were forced to close their doors, while Japan's huge family-controlled industrial combines, known collectively as the *zaibatsu*, consolidated their control of the economy.

Hirohito (visible through window at rear of carriage) rides to his enthronement ceremony in the ancient capital of Kyoto. The enthronement consisted of three days of ancient Shinto rituals. Atop his carriage is a carving of a phoenix, one of the symbols of the imperial dynasty.

The empress Nagako, clad in ceremonial robes for her enthronement with Hirohito in November 1928.

The privations caused by the depression gave rise to the formation of secret, patriotic societies, as the Japanese sought an explanation of and a solution to their economic woes. The members of the patriotic societies were usually small businessmen, farmers, or lower-level army officers — all members of groups that had been frustrated by changes in Japanese society or hurt by the depression. While varying in the particulars, the secret societies shared as their overall credo a belief in an increased role for the military and the need for a "Showa Restoration," anti-Western sentiment, and a growing dislike for parliamentary government and the zaibatsu.

It was obvious to the secret societies that it was party government and the zaibatsu that had led Japan into its current crisis. After all, the zaibatsu had not been hurt by the depression — only small businessmen and farmers, the "real Japanese," had suffered. The emphasis on parliamentary government was an outgrowth of the entire liberalizing, Westernizing trend of Japan's recent history, culminating in the foolishness of the early 1920s, when

63

young Japanese "Mobos" (modern boys) and "Mogos" (modern girls) could be seen walking hand in hand on Tokyo's streets, wearing Western clothes and carrying Oxford bags. As far as the secret societies were concerned, such ways and trends were not Japanese. The adoption of Western ways had only led to confusion, and now disaster. What was needed was a rebirth of traditional Japanese virtues, beginning with loyalty to Showa, the emperor, who must reassert himself and right the nation's course.

The army and navy had grown restive under the constraints placed on it by the government. Because the military had generally opposed the government's policies, the depression had left it untainted politically. As a concession to the spending cuts and the elimination of the four divisions, military training had been introduced into Japan's high and middle schools and was made available to youths not wishing to continue their education. Within the military, conditions were right for the rise of the same type of thinking that characterized the secret societies.

The military continued to be interested in Manchuria, and in September 1931 the army created an incident there as a pretext for invasion. Hirohito (center) is flanked by his brothers Prince Chichibu (left) and Prince Takamatsu (right) at the 30th anniversary celebration of the Japanese army's 1905 victory at Mukden, Manchuria.

Many of the new, younger officers and recruits were from northern Japan, where the depression had been particularly devastating, and they blamed the government and big business for the suffering. Bushido, the code of the warrior, reinforced antipathy toward the zaibatsu — the true samurai disdained contact with the world of commerce. Young officers urged a patriotic devotion to the emperor, who had obviously been misled by his advisers, and argued that it was the military that was best prepared to carry out Hirohito's true wishes and preserve the real Japan.

Much of the anti-Western sentiment was directed at the United States. The United States had been one of the most generous nations in providing relief supplies to Japan following the great earthquake in 1923, but the Japanese were grievously insulted the following year when the U.S. Congress passed a bill setting quotas for immigration into the country. The bill specifically provided that no "Asiatics" be permitted to enter. The Chinese had been excluded by previous legislation; the Japanese rightly assumed that the bill was aimed at them and considered it yet another demonstration of racism on the

When Hirohito became emperor, Prince Saionji Kimmochi (left) was the last surviving genro from the days of Meiji. He became Hirohito's closest adviser, but his warnings about the limits of imperial power and his advice to "reign, not rule" contributed to the young emperor's reluctance to confront the increasingly aggressive military.

The Japanese army's invasion of Manchuria was but one manifestation of Japan's increasing militarism. Between 1930 and 1937 at least four major military plots against the government were uncovered, and the army made use of assassination and its privileges under the constitution to strong-arm the cabinet.

part of the West. The Japanese were further insulted by a 1930 agreement that fixed Japanese naval shipping at a fraction of U.S. and British shipping. Prime Minister Hamaguchi Yoko, who agreed to the treaty, was shot in November 1930 as he stood on a railroad platform in Tokyo.

The assassination attempt was merely a harbinger of bolder actions to follow. In March 1931 several Tokyo army officers, acting with the initial approval of War Minister Ugaki Kazushige, plotted to dissolve the Diet, establish martial law, and install Ugaki as prime minister. Although the plot fell apart at the last moment — probably because Ugaki withdrew his support — the March incident is important because it reveals the growing strength of the militarists and the powerlessness of the government in dealing with them. Several high-level officers were implicated in the plot, including the vice-chief of the general staff (the early right-wing officers had been mostly junior officers), but nothing was done to punish those involved. When the plot was discovered, it was decided that it was best to keep news of the treachery secret. This set a dangerous example for other young officers contemplating actions of their own. One of the conspirators, General Koiso Kuniaki, would become prime minister 13 years later.

With no one willing to reign it in, the army launched a more ambitious scheme. Japan's Kwantung Army (Kwantung was an area on the Liaotung Peninsula) manufactured an incident in September 1931 whereby a Japanese train was blown up near the Manchurian city of Mukden (now known as Shenyang). The Chinese were blamed for the incident, which was used by the army as an excuse to invade and occupy all of Manchuria. This action was taken despite the express disapproval of the war minister and the implied disapproval of Hirohito, who had written to the Japanese commander in Manchuria, urging caution. By the following year the Japanese had installed a former Chinese emperor, Henry Pu-yi, as puppet ruler of the region, renamed it Manchukuo, and were attempting to convince the rest of the world that it was a free state.

The army's action had of course come without the approval of Hirohito, the cabinet, or the Diet. In the days immediately following the September 1931 incident, the Japanese government assured the world that its troops would soon withdraw from the occupied areas. When the invasion continued, the government was made to look duplicitous, but the truth was that the government had been rendered completely powerless to control the military.

Japanese soldiers prepare their meals at the siege of Port Arthur during the Russo-Japanese War. Japan believed it had earned the right to pursue what it saw as legitimate interests in Manchuria by virtue of the blood shed by the 100,000 Japanese soldiers killed or wounded at Port Arthur in 1905.

Popular opinion in Japan regarding the Manchurian action was extremely favorable. The Japanese believed themselves to have a legitimate right to the region, secured by their victory in the Russo-Japanese War and sanctified by the blood of the 100,000 Japanese who had been killed or wounded at Port Arthur. Japanese industry and the military were dependent on the coal, oil, and other natural resources found there. Japan's interests in the region had been secure so long as China remained divided into a number of virtually autonomous fiefdoms under the control of military governors, or warlords, but the recent success of the Nationalist government under Chiang Kai-shek, Sun Yat-sen's successor, in uniting China threatened to upset the status quo. Advocates of the army's action argued that Manchuria could be opened up to Japanese settlers in order to help solve Japan's population problem. (Japan was an extremely crowded nation, which put an enormous strain on its land and resources. In 1920, the United States had a population of 106 million, with a population density of 30 people per square mile. Japan, with a population in 1925 of 64 million, had a population density of more than 400 people to the square mile.) It was further argued that in seizing Manchuria Japan had taken the first step toward creating an Asian empire that, by guaranteeing it access to raw materials and captive trading partners, would enable Japan to withdraw from the world economy and avoid further depressions.

The Nijubashi Bridge leads to the main gate of the imperial palace in Tokyo, a 250-acre complex of buildings, gardens, moats, and parkland.

In October 1931 army officers again plotted to overthrow the government. The plan this time called for the Diet to be bombed from the air while in session. One of the officers involved had second thoughts and exposed the conspiracy, but none of its members was punished.

Hirohito attempted to communicate his displeasure with the military, but his messages, such as the one sent to the commander in Manchuria, were cautious. After the collapse of the government following the October Incident (Japanese governments changed regularly during this period), Hirohito's message to the new prime minister, Inukai Tsuyoshi, concluded: "The army's interference in domestic and foreign politics, and its wilfulness, is a state of affairs which, for the good of the nation, we must view with apprehension." The army's actions were indeed viewed with apprehension, but little could be done to control it.

After giving birth to four daughters (one died in infancy), Nagaka bore to a son and heir to the throne, Akihito, in 1933. From the left are Crown Prince Akihito, Hirohito, Princess Teru, Princess Yori, Prince Yoshi, Nagako, and Princess Taka. The picture was taken in 1936.

Inukai Tsuyoshi, known as the Old Fox, was 75 years old when he became prime minister in 1931. His determination to check the army's belligerence in Manchuria provoked the military's hostility, and he was assassinated in May 1932.

The military did have some tradition of autonomy, as the constitution provided that the army and navy chiefs of staff were answerable only to the emperor. Hirohito's reticence was based on his conception of his role as emperor, which was not, as he saw it, to dictate policy. Both his own temperament and tradition inclined him to concur with whatever the cabinet decided upon. He was more at ease collecting marine specimens than with affairs of state. He depended heavily on his advisers, but by 1932 public opinion had moved far to the right, and intimidated by the right's militancy, few of his advisers advocated a firm hand with the military. Perhaps the great genro of Meiji's era — Ito Hirobumi, Yamagata Aritomo, or Matsukata Masayoshi — would have been equal to the task, but of the genro only Saionji remained.

Inukai was an exception. He was 75 when he took office and not frightened by the threats of the secret societies and the military. He immediately undertook to open negotiations on Manchuria with Chiang Kai-shek, and there is some evidence to suggest that he considered attempting to persuade Hirohito to issue an imperial rescript ordering the army to desist. Naturally, Inukai was not popular with the military, who argued that it was politicians like him who had led Japan to disaster and were continuing to mislead the emperor. True loyalty to the imperial way lay in the army, which would free Hirohito of such false advisers. On May 15, 1932, nine army officers, armed with hand grenades and revolvers, made their way into the prime minister's residence, where they surprised Inukai, his daughter-in-law, and his infant grandchild. He asked them to sit and discuss their views and offered them cigarettes. Instead they opened fire, killing him. The plot had been launched with the approval of the minister of war, Araki Sadao.

Inukai's death brought an end to even the pretense of civilian government. From that point on, the military refused to provide the army, navy, or war minister — without which a government could not be formed — unless the prime minister was either a military officer or would comply with the military's plans.

Throughout these events Hirohito's private life continued to be of concern. Upon his enthronement he had asked that the court concubines and ladies-in-waiting be informed that certain of their services would no longer be required, as he intended to be the first of his long line to remain monogamous. By 1932 Nagako had given birth to three more daughters (one died in infancy), much to the consternation of the courtiers and the public. Saionji, Count Tanaka Mitsuaki, and Count Makino Nabuki, three of the more venerable advisers, sought to persuade Hirohito to have a child by one of the concubines. There was much precedent for such action. Taisho had been Meiji's illegitimate son, and there were many instances of an emperor turning to a concubine when his empress was unable to bear him an heir. Newspapers referred to "the delicate situation at the palace," but Hirohito remained faithful, and soon Nagako was pregnant again. On December 22, 1933, two short blasts on sirens throughout Tokyo announced the joyous news that the empress had given birth to a son. He was named Akihito, but the nation's greater crises were not so easily resolved.

> *The Emperor is a scientist and is an extremely liberal person. He is also a pacifist. Unless we manage to change his mode of thinking somewhat, a deep chasm will divide the emperor and the rightists.*
> —MARQUIS KIDO
> Lord of the Privy Seal,
> in remarks to Hurada

5

Domestic Rebellion and Foreign War

Hirohito continued to try to exert some control over the military. In the aftermath of the assassination of Inukai, Hirohito instructed his advisers to select as prime minister someone "who has no fascist leanings and about whom there has been no unsavory rumour, who is moderate in thought and who is not militaristic." There were few politicians with such qualifications who were willing to fill the position, and the intransigence of the army ensured that the next prime minister would be a military man. Admiral Saito Makoto was chosen.

In China, the Japanese had gradually expanded their presence from Manchuria into the province of Jehol and had taken virtual control of the city of Shanghai. When the League of Nations (an international peacekeeping body established after World War I) objected, Japan withdrew from the League. Hirohito let it be known that the imperial rescript announcing Japan's withdrawal should make the point that the withdrawal was regrettable and that Japan intended to continue to cooperate and maintain relations with other nations. Neither point was to the liking of hard-core militants within the army.

They have killed all of my senior subjects who had served as my hands and feet; they have committed terrible atrocities against these old men. Do such actions conform to the ideal of bushido?
—HIROHITO
on radical rebels in the
Imperial Army, 1936

Japan's military aggression brought it to war with China in 1937 and with the United States, Great Britain, and France in 1941. More than 1.8 million Japanese soldiers lost their lives in World War II. Here, Hirohito visits the Yakusuni Shrine to the war dead in 1952.

A new group of young officers, calling themselves the *Shimpeitai*, or Heaven Sent Troops, prepared to overthrow the government. This time the plot included the assassination of Hirohito, who would be replaced by his brother Prince Chichibu, who was unaware of the plan. Tokyo police learned of the conspiracy and arrested 40 members of the Shimpeitai before they could take action. The constant threat of assassination cost Hirohito the services of Count Makino, who resigned his position as lord keeper of the privy seal (a kind of royal secretary who served as liaison between the emperor, the genro and the advisers, and the government). Although Makino's advice had not always been forceful, there had been no doubt of his loyalty to the emperor.

Professing loyalty to Hirohito, conspirators in the Japanese army assassinated government leaders and took control of central Tokyo in February 1936. Hirohito commanded the mutineers to lay down their arms and then ordered secret courts-martial and executions for many of those involved.

The advocates of a Showa Restoration next seized on the writings of Minobe Tatsukichi, a respected professor of political science at the University of Tokyo. Some years earlier Minobe had written a textbook in which he asserted that the emperor should be and was in fact a constitutional monarch and went on to discuss the emperor as one of several "organs of government." In the political atmosphere of 1935, such statements were regarded as treasonous. The emperor was a deity, above government.

After the assassination of Inukai, the military permitted only military men or civilians favorable to its aims and policies — such as Prince Konoye Fumimaro — to serve as prime minister. During Konoye's two terms, Japan moved closer to war with the United States.

How could Minobe presume to discuss him in such terms? Minobe was vilified in the press, hounded and harassed, forced to resign from the House of Peers, threatened, and shot at. A proclamation was issued outlawing any oral or written statement that suggested the emperor was human, a constitutional monarch, or subject to law. It was forbidden to gaze directly upon him when he traveled in public, and those passing by the imperial palace had to bow toward his presence.

Hirohito of course had no desire to be deified. He had discounted the tales of his divine origin while still a schoolboy, and he deplored the treatment of Minobe, about whom he said: "Much is being said about Minobe; but I do not believe he is disloyal. Just how many men of Minobe's calibre are there in Japan today? It is a pity to consign such a scholar to oblivion."

At the time the army was divided into two factions. One, calling itself the *Kodo-ha*, or Imperial Way School, believed that the Soviet Union posed the greatest threat to Japan's imperial ambitions in Asia. The Kodo-ha contained most of the younger officers obsessed with the Showa Restoration. Its rival, the *Tosei-ha*, or Control School, believed that Japan should expand south from Manchuria into China and Southeast Asia.

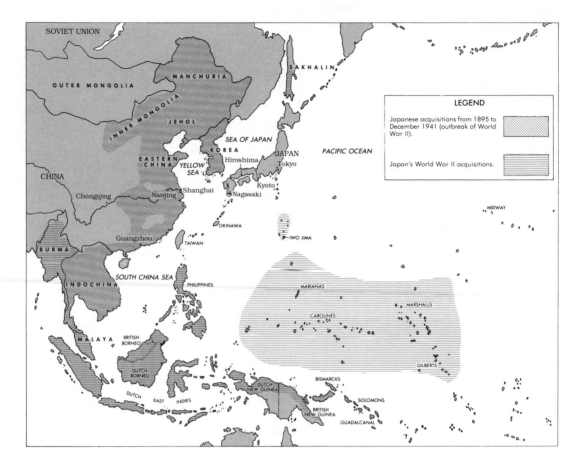

LEGEND

Japanese acquisitions from 1895 to December 1941 (outbreak of World War II).

Japan's World War II acquisitions.

Japan's empire at its greatest extent, shortly after the outbreak of World War II in the Pacific in December 1941.

In the early morning of February 26, 1936, young officers and soldiers of the Japanese army's First Division left their barracks and fanned out through the streets of Tokyo. It had been snowing hard for two days, but the men of the First Division could not afford to wait; they had recently learned that they had been posted to Manchukuo, mainly so that they could no longer incite unrest in the capital. Their targets were the most prominent politicians and advisers in the land; when the morning's shooting was over, former prime ministers Saito and Takahashi Korekiyo had been killed, and the new lord keeper of the privy seal, Saito Makuto, and Suzuki Kantaro, the lord chamberlain, had been wounded. Prime Minister Okada Keisuke escaped death by hiding in a bathroom. The assassins wanted to kill Saionji, but the venerable statesman had sensed trouble and gone into hiding. The 1,500 soldiers involved, none of them above the rank of captain and most of them members of the Kodo-ha, then occupied central Tokyo.

Tokyo's morning newspapers printed the text of a statement given to them that morning by the conspirators. It blamed the genro, the zaibatsu, and party politicians for Japan's problems, describing them as "unrighteous and disloyal creatures who surround the Imperial Throne," and added that it was the soldier's duty to "remove the villains who surround the throne" by killing them.

The occupant of the throne was less than grateful for their concern, and his reaction was quite different from what it had been after the previous coup attempts. The soldiers were nothing other than mutineers, he declared, and the mutiny was immediately suppressed. Leaflets were dropped to the troops, advising them of Hirohito's displeasure and pleading with them to return to their barracks. Other army divisions were called out, and naval forces were brought ashore. (There was considerable interservice rivalry between the army and navy, in some respects paralleling the clan rivalry between Satsuma and Choshu. Although the navy was a participant in the militarization of the government, it

Japanese citizens stand worshipfully at the bridge leading to the imperial palace. The rising nationalism in Japan during the 1930s often took the form of fanatical reverence for the emperor. A new law required passing pedestrians to bow in the direction of the imperial palace.

Hirohito delivers a message to the bowing war minister, Tojo Hideki, in October 1940. One month earlier Hirohito's advisers had persuaded him to approve the Tripartite Pact, which allied Japan with the fascist dictatorships of Adolf Hitler in Germany and Benito Mussolini in Italy.

did not desire to see that government dominated by the army, as would surely be the case if the coup were to succeed. Furthermore, some of those killed were navy officers.) After a four-day standoff, the mutinous troops returned to their barracks, but Hirohito's anger was unabated. The mutineers expected that if punished at all they would be given a public trial, which would present them with an opportunity to further disseminate their views, but the emperor ordered secret courts-martial. Over 100 of the conspirators were tried, and 13 were secretly executed. Hirohito personally approved the sentences. Kita Ikki, a rightist writer and agitator for the Showa Restoration, was also executed. The army chief of staff, Prince Kanin Kotohito, an elderly kinsman of the emperor, assured him that "now the army will be completely reformed, the prerogative of the supreme command will be strengthened, and a national army that is truly united and powerful will be established." It was not to be; the resolve Hirohito had displayed would not be displayed again until it was too late.

The new cabinet, under Hirota Koki, was subordinate to the Tosei-ha faction. Military spending rose to 50 percent of the national budget, the 1921 and 1930 shipping limitations treaties with the United States and Great Britain were abrogated, and Japan embarked on a major arms buildup. The finance minister said in 1936 that Japan's was a "quasi-wartime economy." At the same time steps were taken to make sure that the new militant patriotism was instilled in the hearts and minds of every Japanese. The ministry of education prepared a new book on kokutai and had it distributed throughout the nation's schools and colleges.

In April 1937 Prince Konoye Fumimaro became prime minister. Except for a brief interruption, he was to serve as prime minister until the eve of Japan's entrance into World War II. That he was able to survive so long as prime minister in such tumultuous times attests to his inoffensiveness to the military leaders.

World War II began in Europe in 1939. By the end of 1940 the forces of Hitler (left) controlled most of Europe. Believing that the Tripartite Pact would free the military to pursue its own empire, Hirohito's advisers told him that a treaty with Hitler would mean peace for Japan.

Since the revolution that had overthrown the last of the Qing dynasty emperors, Henry Pu-yi, in 1912, China had experienced a resurgence of nationalist feeling. For years the Chinese had seen their nation exploited economically by a host of foreign powers, who lived under their own laws in virtually independent areas. With its belligerence in Manchuria — treaty concessions were one thing, but armed invasion and occupation were another — Japan became the focus of China's dissatisfaction with its inferior status. Although the Nationalist government under Chiang Kai-shek had been at war with the Chinese Communists under Mao Zedong, both the Communists and the Nationalists agreed on the necessity of fighting the Japanese and tentatively entered into a truce toward that end.

In northern China Japanese and Chinese troops clashed regularly, while in Tokyo the Tosei-ha faction advocated a move into southern China. The Japanese economy was already on a wartime footing; the momentum of years of militarization was moving the nation inexorably toward war. Even Araki, the former war minister and leader of the Kodo-ha, said that the idea of Japan staying out of China was "like telling a man not to get involved with a woman who is already pregnant by him."

The destruction of Nanjing in December 1937 turned the tide of international opinion against Japan. The Japanese believed their brutality against the inhabitants of the former capital of China would induce a quick surrender, but the Chinese continued to resist.

Tojo Hideki helped plan Japan's war with China and served as war minister, prime minister, and army chief of staff during World War II. After Japan's defeat he was tried as a war criminal and hanged in December 1948.

On the night of July 7, 1937, maneuvers by the Japanese army at the Marco Polo Bridge, 15 miles southwest of Beijing (Peking) led to a skirmish with Chinese troops. It remains uncertain who was responsible, although some historians believe that the Japanese intentionally provoked an incident, as they had done at Mukden in 1931, when the demolition of a Japanese train precipitated the crisis in Manchuria. The immediate incident was resolved by the local Japanese and Chinese commanders, but Japanese military men in Tokyo urged that more troops be sent to the area, lest Chiang mistake Japanese restraint for weakness and decide to move on Manchuria. Within days Japanese troops were streaming into the area; Chiang's troops were seen doing the same, and a full-scale war was soon in progress.

The militarists believed that the Chinese would be easily and quickly defeated. On July 27, 1937, Konoye announced that the Japanese policy in China was the imposition of a "new order" for East Asia that would feature the economic, political, and cultural union of Japan, China, and Manchukuo. Shanghai fell to the Japanese in August, and Nanjing (Nanking), Chiang's capital, fell in December 1937. In Nanjing the unleashed Japanese troops

Chinese leader Chiang Kai-shek believed that China's topography and its great size made it unconquerable. After his defeat by the Japanese at Shanghai and his withdrawal from Nanjing he retreated to the interior, content to trade space for time and await the intervention of the United States.

engaged in an orgy of rape, looting, torture, and murder that left over 200,000 Chinese civilians dead. It is probable that the atrocities were carried out with at least the tacit approval of the Japanese commanders and the more radical military leaders in Tokyo, in the belief that the suffering in his former capital would bring home to Chiang the perils of continued resistance, but the Japanese brutality only reinforced the determination of the Chinese to resist.

The confidence of Japanese commanders in the field reached such heights that a U.S. gunship, the USS *Panay*, was shelled and sunk, and a British navy vessel, the HMS *Ladybird*, was attacked and then boarded. Colonel Hashimoto Kingoro, who had been a ringleader in both the March 1931 and October 1931 coups, was responsible. The government was not yet ready to sanction war with Britain and the United States, and Konoye extended hasty apologies and offered the United States reparations for its ship.

Hirohito was kept uninformed about the details of the "China Incident," as the Japanese referred to their war with that nation. He reluctantly acquiesced to the initial Japanese actions there because his cabinet and advisers convinced him they were necessary in order to break Chiang, whose growing strength would ultimately threaten Japanese interests in Manchuria. When it became apparent that there would not be an immediate Japanese victory and that he had been misled as to the extent of the Japanese involvement, he withdrew himself even more than was customary from the government. The details of the Chinese war were kept from him, and it appears he never knew of the Nanjing massacre. The resolve he had shown in quelling the February 1936 mutiny withered; he grew extremely depressed, had trouble sleeping, and appeared haggard and withdrawn. Even his one outlet — his marine biology studies — was denied to him, as the fanatic nationalists determined that his scientific interests were in some way unseemly, and his advisers agreed that it was best he forgo his experiments for the time being.

By the summer of 1938 the Japanese controlled many of China's important cities and the railroads, but they had been unable to secure the countryside, and the Chinese refused to capitulate. Chiang was offered peace, but the terms were as unpalatable as the 21 Demands had been. In the meantime, there were still those within the army who advocated war with the Soviet Union, and they provoked a clash with Soviet troops in the poorly defined border region between Korea, Manchuria, and the Soviet Union. This roused Hirohito, who met with army chief of staff Kanin and War Minister Itagaki Seishiro and told them that the army's past actions had been "abominable." From that point onward, he said, "you may not move one soldier without my command." His words had little effect. The war in China continued, and the following year Japanese troops were routed by the Soviets at Nomonhan, in the border region, which had the effect of permanently discrediting the Kodo-ha faction.

Their success in China inspired the expansionists within the military to contemplate moving Japanese forces into Southeast Asia (present-day Vietnam, Laos, Cambodia, and Thailand) and Malaya and the Dutch East Indies (now Indonesia). By this time, Japanese policy had brought it into direct conflict with the United States.

Japan's designs were not global. Its goal was to establish a pan-Asian empire in the Pacific, and it was largely unconcerned with events in Europe except insofar as those events affected its bid for Asian hegemony. By the end of the 1930s, however, events on the two continents were inextricably linked.

Japan's greatest concern was that another world power or a combination of world powers would step in and put a stop to its expansionism in Asia. After all, the European nations and the United States had long held commercial interests in Asia. Japan primarily feared the intervention of the United States, Great Britain, or the Soviet Union, as only the United States and Great Britain possessed the naval power to challenge the Japanese in the Pacific, and the Soviet Union's proximity made it a threat.

In Europe, dictator Adolf Hitler of Germany had invaded Austria and then seized the Sudetenland, a region of Czechoslovakia. Unprepared for war, Britain, under Prime Minister Neville Chamberlain, had been one of several nations to sign the Munich Pact, which in essence handed over the Sudetenland to Hitler. Hitler's rise effectively eliminated the British as an immediate threat to the Japanese, who correctly determined that if Britain was unprepared to fight in Europe, it was certainly unlikely to intervene in Asia.

That left the United States and the Soviet Union. Japan's aggression in China had brought it into conflict with the United States, whose policy since the turn of the century had been based on maintaining an "open door" in China, meaning that China should remain free to trade and commerce with all nations. (In practice, the Open Door policy had resulted in China being carved into commercial zones dominated by the various world powers.) Japan's new order threatened an end to the open door,

Hirohito's name was invoked by Japan's military leaders as a sanction for all wartime policies. In the United States, where there was little understanding of the limitations on the emperor's power, he was reviled and caricatured as an archvillain and war criminal.

as well as harm to existing U.S. business interests. Furthermore, Chiang was popular in the United States, where his dictatorial tendencies and the corruption of his government had to date gone unreported in the press, which portrayed him as a champion of democracy. Japan had grown increasingly unpopular in the United States since its attempt to impose the 21 Demands in China; the rape of Nanjing, the bombing of civilians in Shanghai, and the attack on the *Panay* earned it more dislike. Even before the attack on the *Panay*, U.S. president Franklin Roosevelt had made a speech in which he likened Japan to Nazi Germany and said that the civilized nations of the world should act together to "quarantine" the aggressor nations by imposing economic embargoes.

The prospect of an economic embargo, particularly one imposed by the United States, was alarming to the Japanese, who relied heavily on imported oil, mainly from the United States. Japanese planners estimated that the nation had enough reserves for only two years. The Dutch East Indies, rich in oil, now became doubly attractive.

By 1939, it was obvious that war in Europe was inevitable. The military favored supporting Germany, in the belief that such an alliance would prevent the Soviet Union from acting against Japan. The cabinet, under Prime Minister Hiranuma Kiichiro, met 70 times on the German question between the summers of 1939 and 1940 but was unable to reach a unanimous decision, mainly because of the opposition of the foreign minister, Arita Hachira, and the navy minister, Yonai Mitsumasa. Both men were still more concerned with the prospect of war with the Soviet Union, and the navy in general was much less reckless than the army. Hirohito and Saionji opposed a treaty with Germany because both were convinced that Great Britain was still going to win the war. In August 1939 the Germans and Soviets signed a treaty of nonaggression with one another. The Japanese were shocked by what they regarded as a betrayal by the Germans, and the immediate result was that the policy of neutrality advocated by Hirohito and Saionji won the day. World War II began the following month with Germany's invasion of Poland. Britain and France immediately declared war on Germany.

In the next year Germany overran Poland, France, the Netherlands, Belgium, Luxembourg, Norway, and Denmark, prompting Japanese army leaders to once again advocate a treaty with Germany and its ally, Italy. A new cabinet, once again under Konoye, agreed to the Tripartite Pact with Germany and Italy. In September 1940 an imperial conference was arranged to obtain Hirohito's approval. The ministers all stated their reasons for supporting the pact. Rather than bringing war with the United States, as they knew the emperor feared the treaty would do, the alliance would bring peace. No longer would Japan have to fear war from the Soviet Union, as the treaty made Japan Germany's ally, and Germany and the Soviet Union had signed a nonaggression pact. Germany was on the verge of defeating Britain, which would leave the United States isolated and unlikely to take action.

Hirohito was unconvinced. He still believed, as did Saionji, that Britain would be victorious. He had every reason to suspect his army ministers when they told him their main concern was peace. But he remained silent. Once again his cabinet was unanimous, and his job, as Saionji had told him many times, was "to reign, not rule." Moreover, his brother, Chichibu, who had become one of his most trusted advisers, was sick and unavailable for counsel, and Saionji was dying. The emperor felt alone and isolated.

The treaty increased tensions between Japan and the United States. In July 1941 Japanese forces moved into France's former colonial possessions in Southeast Asia, and the United States announced an economic embargo. This brought the crisis to a head. Without U.S. oil, Japan had little choice but to attack the Dutch East Indies, and the army had little doubt that such a step would mean war with the United States. The navy had been instructed to develop plans for an assault on the United States and since January had been rehearsing for a surprise attack designed to incapacitate the U.S. Pacific fleet. The idea was to strike the first blow, hold off the United States until it wearied of war, and negotiate an advantageous peace.

Negotiations between the United States and Japan continued, but the two sides were far apart. Japan demanded that the United States withdraw its support for Chiang's government, end the oil embargo, and accept Japanese hegemony in East Asia, in exchange for which it would withdraw from the Tripartite Pact. The United States was willing to settle for nothing less than Japanese withdrawal from China. Roosevelt had made serious efforts to persuade Japan not to move into Southeast Asia, but the impasse between the two nations was now too great.

On September 6, 1941, the most important ministers and advisers again assembled before Hirohito. It had been decided that if negotiations with the United States had not reached a satisfactory end by the middle of October, war would be declared. The delegates all stated their agreement with this policy. As neither the U.S. nor Japanese positions had changed, there was no doubt war would ensue.

On December 7, 1941, Japan launched a surprise attack on the U.S. naval base at Pearl Harbor, Hawaii. The Japanese believed the United States lacked the resolve to pursue a lengthy war to its conclusion.

Hara Yoshimichi was president of the privy council. He complained that the government's decision sounded as if war, not diplomacy, was to be their next resort. The government's ministers did not respond.

Now Hirohito stood up. He had not been expected to speak. Why don't you answer? he asked the delegates, referring to Hara's questions. The military ministers and the chiefs of staff were silent. He was sorry that the supreme command had no answer, he said, and read aloud a poem written by Emperor Meiji:

> All the seas, everywhere,
> are brothers to one another
> Why then do the winds and waves of strife
> rage so violently through the world?

The delegates had no difficulty understanding that the emperor wanted peace. There were a few moments of respectful silence, and then they assured Hirohito that diplomacy would be the first priority. But when the meeting broke up, preparations for war continued. Konoye, who had pushed for a direct meeting with Roosevelt, resigned and was replaced by Tojo Hideki, the war minister. Three months later, on December 7, 1941, came the attack on Pearl Harbor, Hong Kong, Malaya, Singapore, and the Philippines.

Hirohito played a minor role during the war. For the most part he remained in the palace. He made periodic inquiries about the prospects for peace, and his name was invoked by those actually running the war. All public pronouncements were made in the emperor's name. The families of wounded and slain soldiers received condolences from the emperor. One magazine published an article entitled "Revere the Emperor, Expel the Barbarian" (the reference was of course to the battle cry of the 19th-century restorationists) and wrote that "it is neither the State nor the People that declare war . . . the Emperor himself declares war. . . . Accordingly the war will continue until the Emperor says 'cease!' " The U.S. Office of Strategic Services (OSS), an intelligence-gathering agency that was the forerunner of the Central Intelligence Agency (CIA), concluded that the invocation of the emperor's name was a deliberate strategy to "reassure the people of the sacred nature of the war, and that the emperor's divine destiny will assure victory." The OSS also believed that the strategy was designed to force the emperor to share responsibility with the militarists for the war.

Newspaper headline announces the U.S. entrance into World War II. The Japanese strategy was predicated on striking a crippling initial blow and forcing the United States to bargain for peace, but from the outset Roosevelt (pictured) had no intention of negotiating.

Japan's strategic assumptions proved wrong. Hitler attacked the Soviet Union, and the United States entered the war against Germany at the same time as it did against Japan. Germany was successful early, but Allied victories at Stalingrad, in the Soviet Union, and El Alamein, in Egypt, turned the tide. With Italy's surrender in September 1943, it was Germany, not Britain, that was isolated and facing war on two fronts. The war went in much the same fashion for the Japanese. Japan quickly seized a far-flung array of possessions in the Pacific, but the U.S. victory at the island of Midway in the summer of 1942 halted the Japanese advance. Japan's strategy had been predicated on forcing the United States to negotiate a quick peace, but Japan had underestimated the productive capacity of the United States (still recovering from its own depression) and its determination to carry the war to a conclusion. After Midway a U.S. counteroffensive slowly swept west across the Pacific islands, driving the Japanese before them. By the late fall of 1944 U.S. bombers were regularly hitting Japanese cities. On August 6, 1945, the first atomic bomb devastated Hiroshima; three days later Nagasaki was destroyed. Japan's illusory hopes that the Soviet Union would intervene on their behalf had been dashed, and Hirohito assembled the delegates in the obunko and told them that the war was over.

The U.S. victory at Okinawa in July 1945 prepared the way for a planned invasion of the Japanese home islands. But in August 1945 the United States dropped atomic bombs on Hiroshima and Nagasaki, and the Japanese surrendered.

91

6

Reform and Rebirth

September 2, 1945, dawned clear and sunny. In Tokyo Bay, warships from several nations lay at anchor as an armada of aircraft soared overhead. Aboard the USS *Missouri*, Japanese delegates affixed their signatures to the articles of surrender. As U.S. general Douglas MacArthur began his speech, Hirohito was listening on his radio from the imperial library. He had not ventured off the palace grounds since his own historic broadcast three weeks before.

"I speak for the thousands of silent lips, forever stilled among the jungles and the beaches . . . " MacArthur began. "The energy of the Japanese people, if properly directed, will enable expansion vertically rather than horizontally. If the talents of the race are turned into constructive channels, the country can lift itself from the present deplorable state into a position of dignity. To the Pacific basin has come the vista of a new, emancipated world. Today, freedom is on the offensive, democracy is on the march. Today, in Asia as well as in Europe, unshackled peoples are tasting the full sweetness of liberty, the relief from fear."

Their whole world has crumbled. It is not merely the disintegration of everything they believed in and lived by and fought for, but they were left a complete vacuum, morally, mentally, and physically.
—GENERAL DOUGLAS MACARTHUR commenting on Japan after the peace treaty

The ruins of a building damaged by the atomic bomb in Hiroshima are preserved as a memorial amid the gleaming high rises that testify to Japan's rebirth in the years following the nuclear devastation.

Planes of the Allied powers fly above the U.S. fleet in Tokyo Bay on September 2, 1945 — the day Japanese delegates signed the surrender documents on board the USS *Missouri*, ending World War II.

The Pacific war had been waged for four years. The ceremony ushering in a new era of cooperation lasted precisely 18 minutes.

MacArthur had been given almost unlimited authority to conduct the occupation as he saw fit. Imperious in manner, a student of history and of Japan, he was convinced that it was his destiny to play a historic role in the rebirth of Japan. He believed that the responsibility for Japan's aggression rested with its leaders, who had conspired to lead it to war, but that this had been made possible by the feudal nature of Japanese society and the reactionary character of its political system. Japan would have to be disarmed, the empire dissolved, its leadership purged, the political system democratized, State Shinto disestablished, and the zaibatsu busted.

MacArthur established his Tokyo headquarters in the Dai-Ichi Building, across from the imperial palace. On September 26 Hirohito dispatched his foreign minister to request permission to make a formal call on the general. MacArthur arranged a meeting for that afternoon at the American embassy. He was still unsure about how to treat Hirohito. Opinions about the exact extent of the emperor's role were divided. Some believed that Hirohito was as guilty as any of the other Japanese leaders and ought to be prosecuted as a war criminal, while others felt he had been no more than a figurehead and bore little responsibility. MacArthur himself leaned toward the idea that the emperor could be useful in easing the Japanese transition to democracy and believed that to prosecute him would make him a martyr in Japanese eyes and stiffen resistance to the occupation's reforms. The Soviet Union wanted Hirohito tried, and the Australians, who as members of the British Commonwealth had done the majority of Britain's Pacific fighting, were particularly adamant in their insistence that Hirohito was a war criminal.

The seal of the Japanese empire (in center square) and the signature of Hirohito (above seal) on one of the surrender documents. Hirohito did not attend the surrender ceremony.

MacArthur said later that he was prepared to be "stern" with Hirohito at their first meeting. Wearing baggy, pinstriped trousers and a top hat, the emperor arrived in his old Rolls-Royce and marched bravely into the embassy to meet the general. "I met him cordially," MacArthur wrote, "and recalled that I had at one time been received by his father at the close of the Russo-Japanese War. He was nervous and the stress of the past months showed plainly. I offered him an American cigarette, which he took with thanks [this despite the fact that Hirohito had never smoked]. I noticed how his hands shook as I lighted it for him. I tried to make it as easy for him as I could, but I knew how deep and dreadful must be his agony of humiliation.

Foreign Minister Shigemitsu Mamoru signs the surrender documents aboard the *Missouri*. He was greatly impressed by the magnanimity shown the representatives of the vanquished Japanese by the Allies.

"What he said was this," the general wrote, "'I come to you, General MacArthur, to offer myself to the judgment of the powers you represent as the one to bear sole responsibility for every political and military decision made and action taken by my people in the conduct of the war.' A tremendous impression swept me. This courageous assumption of a responsibility implicit with death, a responsibility clearly belied by facts of which I was fully aware, moved me to the very marrow of my bones."

MacArthur instantly cabled President Harry Truman that the emperor was not to be subjected to a trial or any other forum to establish guilt, to which Truman reluctantly agreed. During the trials that followed, Togo and Tojo were among those convicted. Konoye took poison rather than face trial.

Hirohito, wearing mourning clothes, meets with U.S. general Douglas MacArthur in 1945. MacArthur directed the Allied occupation of Japan. He recommended that Hirohito not be tried as a war criminal after hearing him assume responsibility for the war, but the emperor's role was reduced to a symbolic one.

97

Hirohito remained popular with his countrymen after Japan's defeat, and Mac-Arthur encouraged him to travel around the nation to promote cooperation with the reforms instituted during the occupation.

MacArthur considered it extremely important that State Shinto, with its myths of the divine origins of the emperor, be brought to an end. He believed that the militarists had cleverly utilized such doctrines to ensure the allegiance of the Japanese people to the emperor, ensuring at the same time support for their own misguided policies, which ostensibly had imperial approval. At Mac-Arthur's insistence, Hirohito's New Year's Day rescript of 1946 asserted that "the ties between [the emperor] and our people have always stood upon mutual trust and affection" and were not "predicated on the false conception that the emperor is divine."

MacArthur then encouraged the emperor to make trips around the devastated countryside, to survey the damage and encourage rebuilding efforts. On the first of these he was shy and constantly fumbled his words, managing only an *ah, so desu ka*?" ("Is that so?") or two. But the nervousness was soon replaced by a smile, a wave with his trademark gray hat, and a comfortable interview style. The Japanese loved their emperor's new, accessible incarnation. When word got out that 6,000 of the emperor's retainers had been dismissed and the palace gardens had become badly overgrown, thousands of volunteers appeared at the palace to landscape the vast grounds.

When MacArthur cut the imperial budget and Hirohito was no longer able to retain the servants necessary to maintain the palace grounds, volunteers offered their services.

During the war years Hirohito's advisers felt it was improper for the emperor to pursue his consuming interest in marine biology, and Hirohito complied with their wishes. After the war, however, he resumed his studies, eventually publishing several books on the subject.

Meanwhile, the demilitarization and democratization of Japan proceeded. The armed forces were dismantled by 1946; political reforms began in 1945 and culminated with the Diet's ratification of a new constitution in 1947, which retained the emperor as "the symbol of the State and of the unity of the people" but proclaimed that "sovereign power resides with the people." The new constitution ended State Shinto and provided for the equality of the sexes, legalized labor unions, partial dissolution of the zaibatsu, and extensive reforms in the systems of land ownership, police authority, and general educational practices. Article 9 renounced the nation's right to use the threat of force, to maintain armed forces, and to make war. Within weeks of the outbreak of the Korean War in 1950, however, Japan was called on to create a paramilitary force for the maintenance of internal security. These troops, known as the Self-Defense Forces, remain the nation's only trained fighters.

The International Military Tribunal for the Far East, established in 1948 in Tokyo, tried and sentenced to death or imprisonment 25 Japanese officers and leaders for their roles in the war effort; 4,000 more were tried by other tribunals. In 1950 the occupation was terminated, and Japan's independence was restored. Most Japanese were impressed by the magnanimity of the victors. The physical and spiritual desolation of seven years earlier had been almost completely eradicated, replaced by a rejuvenated, revitalized Japan on the brink of an economic miracle.

Between 1954 and 1967 Japan's gross national product grew at a rate of 10.1 percent, faster than any other national economy during the period. The government showed itself willing to collaborate in private ventures and was especially supportive of industries with the potential of developing export capacity. By 1963 Japan's economy had become the third largest in the world. Two years later, just twenty years after the war had left its economy in a shambles, Japan had its first trade surplus.

Since World War II Japan has rebuilt its economy. Japanese cars and electronic goods are exported around the world, but Japan remains dangerously dependent on imports for the mineral resources — particularly oil — that fuel its industry.

Hirohito and Nagako lived quietly during the decades following the war, making only occasional public appearances and foreign visits. This medal was cast to commemorate their 1971 visit to France.

Problems remain. Japan's population reached 125 million by the mid-1980s, increasing overcrowding, pollution, and land and housing shortages. Security remains an issue, with many arguing that the lack of armed forces leaves Japan vulnerable, particularly with regard to the Soviet Union. Its economic success has led to difficulties. Japan's emphasis on exports derives partly out of necessity; export income is badly needed because Japan still must import most of its raw materials. Japan remains almost entirely dependent on imports of oil and other energy sources. A bestseller written during the Arab oil embargo of 1973—74 estimated that if the country's oil imports were cut off for just 200 days, more than half of its businesses would go bankrupt, 30 million people would lose their jobs, and 3 million people would die. Nevertheless, Japan's success with exports, particularly with its main trading partner, the United States, has led to complaints about its aggressive trade practices abroad and its protectionist trade legislation at home. The enormous success of the Japanese steel, electronics, and auto-manufacturing exports enabled it to enjoy a $60 billion trade surplus with the United States in 1987, leading to calls in that nation for legislation that would restrict Japanese exports.

Japan has normalized its foreign relations in the years since the war, developing diplomatic ties with over 150 nations. Its closest ally is the United States, which looks to Japan as one of the few stable democracies in the Far East. Relations with the Chinese were virtually nonexistent in the years following the war; the Japanese were shocked when U.S. president Richard Nixon normalized relations with the Chinese in 1972 — the United States and China had broken off relations in 1949, after Mao Zedong's Communist forces defeated Chiang's Nationalists — but the following year the Japanese followed suit. Prime Minister Tanaka Kakuei visited China and apologized for Japan's war crimes, and a treaty of friendship was signed in 1978.

During the decades following the war, Hirohito and Nagako led quiet, unassuming lives out of public view, making only occasional appearances at important events, such as the Olympic Games held in Japan in 1964 and 1972. The emperor held his first and last press conference — at which he was not particularly candid — in 1965. In 1968, he and Nagako moved into a new imperial palace, where they continued to spend time together as they had for many years — reading, watching television, taking frequent strolls about the palace grounds, and hosting their seven children and dozens of grandchildren

Hirohito stated that his 1975 visit to the United States was the culmination of a long-time desire. He was invited to Disneyland, where he was photographed with Mickey Mouse.

The imperial family. From left, front: Hirohito, Prince Aya and Prince Hiro (grandchildren), and Nagako. At rear are Crown Prince Akihito, Crown Princess Michiko (holding Princess Nori), Princess Hitachi, and Prince Hitachi (son).

and great-grandchildren during their regular visits to the palace. Though in 1970 the imperial couple made an 18-day goodwill tour of 7 European countries, this was a rare venture out of the palace and an even rarer venture out of the country for Hirohito and Nagako, who clearly preferred their privacy to public life.

On certain other occasions the imperial couple stepped into public view. Each year on New Year's Day and on April 29, the emperor's official birthday, the palace grounds were opened. Hundreds of thousands of Japanese came to get a glimpse of the emperor and his family waving to them from behind the windows of a room designed to make them visible to, yet insulated from, the throngs. The festivities included the waving of the Japanese flag, which depicts a red sun on a sea of white. Cries of *"Banzai!"* ("One thousand cheers!") were usually audible.

Hirohito continued his research in the field of marine biology. His first publication, *The Opisthobranchia of Sagami Bay*, appeared in 1949. He wrote a dozen subsequent books on marine biology and was eventually recognized as a leading authority in his field.

Hirohito also indulged in literary pastimes. He penned hundreds of *haiku* (3-line, 17-syllable poems) and *tanka* (5-line, 31-syllable poems). It became customary each New Year's Day for the emperor to read his poetry at a special ceremony. Hirohito kept a diary from the age of 12, but it is uncertain whether its contents will ever be made available to the public. Historians certainly hope that they are granted access to the emperor's diary, for it might reveal much about the man and his times.

In September 1988, the 87-year-old Hirohito became seriously ill and was hospitalized. He was anemic and had experienced internal bleeding. Pancreatic surgery revealed that the emperor had cancer. Though he remained bedridden for months, Hirohito was never told how serious his condition was. (In Japan, patients with terminal illnesses are generally not told the truth about their condition but are instead allowed to spend their last days clinging to whatever little hope remains.) Hirohito, Japan's longest-reigning monarch, died in Tokyo on January 7, 1989.

A period of national mourning followed the official announcement of Hirohito's death. Perhaps it is difficult for a westerner to comprehend the profound national loss the Japanese felt on this occasion. Millions of Japanese people paid their respects at the gates of the imperial palace, signed an official condolence register, and tried to comfort each other. Unable to cope with their grief, several individuals took their own lives in the days following the announcement. The emperor's funeral was scheduled for February 24.

The international reaction to Hirohito's death was mixed: Many world leaders, including U.S. president Ronald Reagan and Britain's queen Elizabeth II, sent official notices of condolence to the widowed empress and the Japanese government, whereas others marked the occasion by criticizing Hirohito's role in World War II. British World War II veterans urged Prime Minister Margaret Thatcher to boycott the funeral. New Zealand's defense minister, Bob Tizzard, went so far as to say that Hirohito "should

The grounds of the imperial palace were opened to the public on April 29, 1986, when Hirohito officially celebrated his 85th birthday and the 60th anniversary of his accession to the throne. With him is Nagako.

have been shot or publicly chopped up at the end of the war," and no condolences were expressed by the New Zealand government.

The funeral, which cost the Japanese government $25 million, drew some 700 foreign dignitaries from 160 nations. Among the leaders present were newly inaugurated U.S. president George Bush, François Mitterand of France, Richard von Weizsacker of West Germany, King Juan Carlos I of Spain, King Hussein of Jordan, and Prince Nawaf bin Abdul Aziz al-Saud of Saudi Arabia. Prince Philip, the duke of Edinburgh, represented Great Britain at the funeral. Anatoly Ivanovich Lukyanov, first vice chairman of the Presidium of the Supreme Soviet, represented the Soviet Union. More than 200,000 people lined the procession route, and Japan observed a minute of silence at noon. The empress, herself ill, did not attend the ceremonies.

Until his death on January 7, 1989, Hirohito remained an enigmatic figure. Though Hirohito never spoke publicly about his role in the great events of modern Japanese history, historians hope that his diary will give them greater insight into his eventful reign.

For historians, Hirohito's life remains surrounded by mystery and controversy. Some maintain that even if Hirohito was not in total control of the events leading up to Japan's involvement in World War II, he was guilty of complicity in failing to move forcefully to condemn Japan's militarism. Many other historians disagree with such views. In part the differing interpretations are due to the difficulty of understanding the singular nature of the Japanese institution of the emperor — a divine monarch granted absolute power and regarded as the high priest of a nation's state religion, yet forbidden to rule. Another difficulty is that the Japanese have shown little inclination to examine their wartime conduct, and many important records of the World War II period have yet to be released. It will be some time, even if the contents of Hirohito's diary are made public, before historians will be able to come to a full understanding of the Japanese emperor's role in the war.

Hirohito's 55-year-old son Akihito ascended the Chrysanthemum Throne on January 7, only hours after his father's death, becoming Japan's 125th emperor. The next day he officially began his reign, known as the era of Heisei, or Achieving Peace. On the same day, Akihito's son Hiro became Crown Prince Naruhito so that future generations in Japan, like their ancestors, would hear the voice of the crane.

Further Reading

Bergamini, David. *Japan's Imperial Conspiracy.* New York: Morrow, 1971.

Hane, Mikiso. *Emperor Hirohito and His Chief Aide-de-Camp: The Honjo Diary.* Tokyo: University of Tokyo Press, 1982.

Iyor, Pico, and Michael Walsh. "The Longest Reign: With Hirohito's Death, an Economic Giant Begins a New Era". *Time,* 16 January 1989.

Kanroji, Osanaga. *Hirohito: An Intimate Portrait of the Japanese Emperor.* Los Angeles: Gateway, 1975.

"The Last of Hirohito, the Last of an Era". *U.S. News & World Report,* 16 January 1989.

Manning, Paul. *Hirohito: The War Years.* New York: Dodd, Mead, 1986.

Morganthau, Tom. "Death of an Emperor; It Was the Worst of Times, It Was the Best of Times." *Newsweek,* 16 January 1989.

Mosley, Leonard. *Hirohito: Emperor of Japan.* Englewood Cliffs, NJ: Prentice-Hall, 1966.

Packard, Jerrold H. *Sons of Heaven: A Portrait of the Japanese Monarchy.* New York: Scribners, 1987.

Reischauer, Edwin O. *Japan: The Story of a Nation.* New York: Knopf, 1974.

———. *The Japanese.* Cambridge: Harvard University Press, 1977.

Storry, Richard. *A History of Modern Japan.* New York: Penguin, 1984.

Tasker, Peter. *The Japanese.* New York: Dutton, 1988.

Young, Morgan. *Imperial Japan: 1926–38.* London: Allen & Unwin, 1938.

Chronology

April 29, 1901	Hirohito is born
Feb. 1904	Russo-Japanese War begins
Aug. 1905	Treaty of Portsmouth ends war and establishes Japan as world power
July 29, 1912	Emperor Meiji dies; Yoshito inherits the throne
Sept. 9, 1912	Hirohito officially proclaimed heir to the throne
1914	Imperial Palace School established
	World War I begins
1918	World War I ends
March–Sept. 1921	Hirohito visits Europe
Dec. 27, 1923	Labor activist fails in attempt on Hirohito's life
Dec. 26, 1926	Yoshito dies
Dec. 28, 1926	Hirohito christens his reign as "Showa" (enlightened peace)
Nov. 1928	Officially declared 124th emperor of Japan
Feb. 26, 1936	Mutinous uprising of soldiers trying to kill Hirohito is crushed
July 7, 1937	Chinese and Japanese troops clash at Marco Polo Bridge, setting off Sino-Japanese War
Sept. 1940	Japan, Germany, and Italy sign the Tripartite Pact
Dec. 7, 1941	Japan attacks Pearl Harbor, Hong Kong, Malaya, Singapore, and the Philippines
	United States declares war on Japan
Aug. 6, 1945	United States drops atomic bomb on Hiroshima
Aug. 9, 1945	United States drops atomic bomb on Nagasaki
Aug. 15, 1945	Hirohito addresses Japan on radio, announces surrender
Sept. 2, 1945	Japanese delegates sign surrender aboard the *Missouri*
Sept. 26, 1945	Hirohito meets MacArthur to plan new course for Japan
1947	New constitution retains emperor as symbol of unity
1964	Hirohito attends Olympic Games held in Tokyo
1968	Moves into new imperial palace
1970	Makes 18-day goodwill tour of Europe
1972	Attends Olympic Games held in Tokyo
September 1988	Becomes ill and is hospitalized
January 7, 1989	Dies of cancer in Tokyo

Index

Karen Severns holds an M.S. in journalism from the University of Illinois. As a stafff reporter for the *Asahi Evening News* and the *Asahi Weekly* in Tokyo, she published numerous articles and reviews. Most recently she was associate director of publications for the American Council for the Arts, before taking up permanent residence in Japan.

Arthur M. Schlesinger, jr., taught history at Harvard for many years and is currently Albert Schweitzer Professor of the Humanities at City University of New York. He is the author of numerous highly praised works in American history and has twice been awarded the Pulitzer Prize. He served in the White House as special assistant to Presidents Kennedy and Johnson.

PICTURE CREDITS

AP/Wide World Photos: pp. 12, 15, 25, 69, 70, 74, 77, 80, 81, 91, 94, 95, 98, 99, 100, 102, 103, 105;   Black Star: p. 101;   Culver Pictures: pp. 21, 24, 37, 47, 48;   Dennis Cowels/Black Star: p. 107;   Donna Sinisgalli: p. 76;   Japan Information Center: pp. 2, 68, 104;   L'Illustration/Sygma: pp. 55, 57, 60;   New York Public Library Picture Collection: pp. 34, 85;   Panaphoto/Black Star: pp. 30, 31, 32, 63;   Philip Jones Griffiths/Magnum: p. 92;   Rene Burri/Magnum: p. 41;   Sekai Bunka: pp. 14, 22, 38;   The Bettmann Archive: pp. 18, 19, 29, 33, 35, 36, 39, 43, 46, 50, 53, 62, 66, 67, 72, 82, 88, 89, 90, 96, 97;   Toshi Matsumoto/Sygma: p. 106;   UPI/Bettmann Newsphotos: pp. 16, 17, 20, 28, 44, 49, 52, 64, 65, 75, 78;   Verlag/Blackstar: p. 79;   Werner Bischof/Magnum: pp. 26, 40